Fr. Robert J. Kus

FLOWERS IN THE WIND 2

Story~Based Homilies for Cycle C

RED LANTERN PRESS
WILMINGTON, NORTH CAROLINA

Also by Red Lantern Press

Journals by Fr. Robert J. Kus
- Dreams for the Vineyard: Journal of a Parish Priest - 2002
- For Where Your Treasure Is: Journal of a Parish Priest – 2003
- There Will Be Your Heart Also: Journal of a Parish Priest - 2004

Homily Collections by Fr. Robert J. Kus
- Flowers in the Wind 1 – Story-Based Homilies for Cycle B
- Flowers in the Wind 2 – Story-Based Homilies for Cycle C

ISBN: 1500189792
ISBN-13: 9781500189792

Red Lantern Press, Wilmington, North Carolina
Printed by CreateSpace,
An Amazon.com Company

redlanternpress.com

Dedication

To Chris & Bruce Isler

of

Canton, Ohio

Acknowledgments

Many thanks go to Nolan Heath and Pat Marriott of the Basilica Shrine of St. Mary in Wilmington, N.C. who helped with the editing of these homilies.

Many thanks also go to the parishioners of both St. Catherine of Siena Parish in Wake Forest, N.C. and the Basilica Shrine of St. Mary for whom I originally created these homilies.

Table of Contents

Introduction

TABLE OF CONTENTS

Introduction

The purpose of this book is to provide Catholic preachers a complete collection of homilies for Cycle C. Though it is designed specifically for Catholic priests, the homilies should prove useful for preachers in other mainstream Christian denominations as well.

Each homily starts with the Sunday of the Year being celebrated followed by the Scripture selection that is being discussed. This is followed by a story that appeals for people of all ages. Finally, each homily then discusses the concepts that can be gleaned from the Scripture and story and how we can apply them to our everyday lives.

Each homily takes less than eight minutes. This is especially important for preachers who are in parishes that have Masses every 90 minutes and have to get parking lots filled and emptied in a limited amount of time.

The homilies were created while I was pastor of parishes with large concentrations of children. I'm happy to say the stories make the homilies vibrant and interesting, and families love talking about the stories during the week.

Preachers may take the homilies whole, or they may tweak them to fit their specific needs.

Every effort has been made to credit the authors of each story. In the event that this was not possible, the stories are listed as being written by "Anonymous."

Part 1

ADVENT &
CHRISTMAS SEASONS

Chapter 1

1st Sunday of Advent - C
Living Tomorrows Today

Scripture:

- Jeremiah 33: 14-16
- Psalm 25: 4-5, 8-9, 10 & 14
- 1 Thessalonians 3: 12 - 4: 2
- Luke 21: 25-28, 34-36

Today, we begin a new Church Year, Year C – the Year of St. Luke. That means that for the most part, each week when we come to celebrate the Sunday Eucharist, we'll be hearing from the Gospel of St. Luke.

We begin this new Church Year with the Season of Advent, a season of "joyful expectation." The first two weeks of Advent focus on the coming of Christ at the end of time, while the second two weeks of Advent focus on the coming of the Christ Child on Christmas.

The theme of this Sunday is living our lives in such a way that we will be ready for the coming of Christ at the end of time. Specifically, in St. Paul's First Letter to the Thessalonians, we hear that we are to "abound in love for one another" and be "blameless in holiness."

In the Gospel selection from St. Luke, we hear, "Don't become drowsy from carousing and drunkenness and anxieties of daily life."

Embedded in these Scripture selections is the idea that we are to fully live each day with purpose. Unfortunately, many people fail to live up to these ideas because they procrastinate. They fall into a habit of putting things off until tomorrow.

The following essay, called "Tomorrow," captures this sentiment.

"Tomorrow"
By
Anonymous

He was going to be all that he wanted to—Tomorrow.
None would be kinder or braver than he—Tomorrow.
A friend who was troubled and weary, he knew,
Who'd be glad of a life, and who needed it too,
On him he would call and see what he could do...
    Tomorrow.
Each morning he stacked up the letters he'd write...
    Tomorrow.
And thought of the folks he would fill with delight...
    Tomorrow.
But hadn't one minute to stop on his way,
"More time I will give to others," he'd say...Tomorrow.
The greatest of disciples this man would have been...

Tomorrow.
The world would have hailed him if he had seen…
Tomorrow.
But, in fact, he passed on, and he faded from view,
And all that he left here when living was through,
Was a mountain of things he intended to do…Tomorrow.

This little essay is an excellent one for today, because it talks about one of the most common blocks to a healthy spirituality - procrastination. And this is especially deadly when we consider that our time here on Earth is limited, and we are accountable for how we are living our lives each day at a time. Therefore, it is worthwhile to take a look at this particular vice.

Procrastination is putting off things that we are supposed to be doing. Frequently, this means that we put off important tasks with less important ones. I had a colleague when I taught at The University of Iowa who told me that whenever it was her turn to prepare to deliver a major lecture, she would have a mad desire to clean her house. Housecleaning was her primary method of procrastination.

But, the bigger question is, why do we procrastinate? If we could figure that out, we could be more likely to combat this vice and replace it with the virtue of hard work or perseverance. Here are three likely causes of procrastination:

First, we procrastinate because what we need to do is not as much fun as something else. Playing soccer after school when we should be doing math problems for homework is a good example. As human beings, we are always tempted to do things which please us before doing things we consider a drudgery.

Second, people procrastinate because they don't know how to do something. Faced with a task that they believe is over their head, they simply keep putting it off. Simply admitting that they don't know how to do something, and then asking for help, is a simple way of combatting procrastination based on a lack of knowledge.

And third, sometimes people are perfectionists, and this leads to procrastination. When I first became a professor in a publish-or-perish university, a very prolific writer told me that the "kiss of death" for a professor—or any writer—was to be a perfectionist. "Just write!" she told me. "You can always edit what you have written, but you can't edit a blank piece of paper." She was so correct. There is no perfect book or perfect article or perfect cake or perfect house or perfect anything here on earth. Everything could be better. So what! Get over it. Jump into life and give it your best shot. So it's not perfect? Welcome to the human race!

As we begin our Advent journey this week, it would be a good idea to examine our own lives. How is procrastination blocking our spiritual path? What are some of the ways we can counteract this?

And that is the good news I have for you on this First Sunday of Advent.

Story Source: "Tomorrow." *Sower's Seeds of Encouragement: Fifth Planting*, Ed. Brian Cavanaugh. New York: Paulist Press, 1998. #68, p. 64.

Chapter 2

2nd Sunday of Advent - C
Mother Antonia & Growth

Scripture:

- Baruch 5: 1-9
- Psalm 126: 1-2ab, 2cd-3, 4-5, 6
- Philippians 1: 4-6, 8-11
- Luke 3: 1-6

Today, Catholic Christians celebrate the Second Sunday of Advent, and we encounter one of my very favorite Bible passages. In his letter to the Philippians, Paul says, "I am confident of this, that the one who began a good work in you will continue to complete it until the day of Christ Jesus" (Philippians 1: 6). This means that God is not done with us, that we still have growing to do. What a comforting and exciting idea this is!

In the following story, we hear how one woman opened herself up to God's work in her and, as a result, went on to do great things.

Mary Clarke was born into an Irish Catholic family and raised in an expensive neighborhood in Beverly Hills, California. Her family, though wealthy, did not neglect the poor and marginalized of society. In fact, Mary and her family helped in various projects that reflected Catholic social teaching such as sending health care supplies to poor nations and providing help to the United Farm Workers movement.

When she grew up, Mary became a wife and mother. Her two marriages, in which she produced seven children, ended in divorces.

While she was raising children, Mary ran her deceased father's business and was very active in charitable activities. Such a feat shows the amazing energy, dedication, and organizational skills God gave her. She took the gifts God gave her and put them into action.

But after 25 years of marriage, and after her children were mostly raised and on their own, Mary felt a special call from God. To answer the call, Mary sold her home and possessions and began working at the notorious La Mesa Penitentiary in Tijuana, Baja California, Mexico.

After receiving permission to take private vows as a Sister, Mary put on a religious habit and became known as Sister Antonia. After working a year in the penitentiary, Bishop Juan Jesús Posadas of Tijuana and Bishop Leo Maher of the neighboring American Diocese of San Diego, formally welcomed her and blessed the work she was doing.

In time, Sr. Antonia founded a new religious congregation composed of older women. The new Order is called the Eudist Servants of the Eleventh Hour. Antonia became known as Mother Antonia as head of this Order, and the Sisters have a special love for St. John Eudes, a 17th Century French priest who was also a nurse and missionary. The "Eleventh Hour" comes from the Gospel of Matthew, and it refers to those called to work in the vineyard at the end of the day. In the context of Mother Antonia's

Order, it refers to those who are called later in life to devote themselves in a special way to serve the Lord.

In her life, Mother Antonia lives with the women in prison in a 10 x 10 foot cell. She spends her days visiting with the prisoners and providing spiritual guidance to the guards and prisoners and prisoners' families. Because she is so loved by all, she has never had to worry about her safety.

Mother Antonia also helps the prisoners by providing basic necessities such as medicines and blankets and toiletries.

In 2007, the road to La Mesa Penitentiary was changed from "Los Pollos" (The Chickens) to "Madre Antonia" in honor of "The Prison Angel." In 2010, a documentary on Madre Antonia's life called, "La Mama: An American Nun in a Mexican Prison" was produced and released. It took five years to make. She is also the subject of a book by Mary Jordan and Kevin Sullivan called *The Prison Angel: Mother Antonia's Journey from Beverly Hills to a Life of Service in a Mexican Jail*.

Now, when we hear stories about people such as Mother Antonia, we may think that while they are indeed quite inspirational, they have little to do with us "ordinary" people. But that is far from true. Stories about any human being can teach us about ourselves, and stories of amazing people can teach us even more than most.

From the Scripture passage that we started with today about how the work that God began in us will continue to be developed, and from the life of Mother Antonia, we can glean many things. Here are just three:

First, life implies growth. Without growth, there is no life, there's only existence and death. This principle applies to all human life at all ages. Today, for example, we see a woman becoming a Religious Sister at the age of 50. The important principle here is that growth should not stop simply because one is older.

Second, some growth is very easy to see, while other kinds of growth are more difficult to see. We can easily see intellectual growth of children, for example, as they progress through school. Each year they learn more and more in the same field and in different fields. As we get older, growth is usually not as dramatic except in cases like Mother Antonia.

And third, growth can show up in very small things. Some people have difficulty saying things such as "I love you" or "I was wrong" or "I am sorry" or "I don't know." There is a clever commercial on TV right now where one man says he's "99.9 percent sure" about something. The other man says, "So, you don't know." That's true; if you're not 100 percent sure, you don't know. But growth occurs when a person begins to use these phrases he or she never used before. To them, it is a very big breakthrough in growth, but others may not even realize something new has happened.

As we continue our life journey this week, it would be a good idea to reflect on how we are growing as human beings. What are the blocks to our growth?

And that is the good news I have for you on this Second Sunday of Advent.

Story Source: Jane Jordan. *The Prison Angel: Mother Antonia's Journey from Beverly Hills to a Life of Service in a Mexican Jail.* New York: Penguin Press, 2005.

Chapter 3

3rd Sunday of Advent - C
A Simple Gesture Saves a Life

Scripture:

- Zephaniah 3: 14-18a
- Isaiah 12: 2-3, 4bcd, 5-6
- Philippians 4: 4-7
- Luke 3: 10-18

Today, Catholic Christians celebrate the Third Sunday of Advent, sometimes called "Gaudete Sunday," the Sunday of Joy. This is one of the two Sundays of the year when priests may wear rose-colored vestments, and this is the day we light the rose-colored candle of our Advent wreaths.

In all of the readings for today, we hear about various virtues that we should cultivate, specifically joy, kindness, thanksgiving, generosity, honesty, truthfulness, and being satisfied with what we have. In this homily, we will look at the virtue of kindness.

Kindness is often defined as the state of being gentle, friendly, tenderhearted, generous, sympathetic, or cordial towards other people.

One of the most amazing things about this particular virtue is that we have unlimited opportunities to practice it in our daily lives whether at home, at work, at stores, at school, or wherever we are.

If we are in the habit of being kind towards others, we frequently do not see its effects. People who deal with us are used to us acting in a kind way. But, sometimes, acts of kindness can have a profound effect on others - an effect that we cannot even imagine unless they are pointed out to us. That is indeed what we see in the inspirational story by John Wayne Schlatter.

One day, Mark was walking home from school. A boy who was walking ahead of him tripped and dropped all of the books he was carrying along with a tape recorder, a couple of sweaters, a baseball bat, and a baseball glove. Mark knelt down and helped the boy pick up his scattered belongings. Because they were walking the same way, Mark decided to help the other boy carry his belongings.

As they walked along, Mark learned that the other boy's name was Bill. He also learned that Bill loved video games, baseball, and history. He also learned that Bill was having a lot of trouble in his other subjects and had just broken up with his girlfriend. They got to Bill's house first, and Bill invited Mark in for a soft drink and to watch some television. The boys enjoyed each other's company and the afternoon passed pleasantly.

The boys continued to see each other around school, and they had lunch together once or twice. They ended up at the same high school where they had brief contacts over the years. Finally, they were getting ready to be high school graduates.

Three weeks before graduation, Bill asked Mark if they could talk. Bill reminded Mark of the day years earlier when they had first met.

Bill asked, "Did you ever wonder why I was carrying so many things from school that day? You see, I had cleaned out my locker because I didn't want to leave a mess for anyone else. I had saved up a lot of my mother's pills and I was on my way home to commit suicide. But after you helped me pick up my things, and after we had spent the afternoon together, I realized that if I committed suicide, I would have missed that time and many other good times like it. So you see, Mark, when you helped me pick up my books for me that day, you did a lot more. You saved my life."

What a remarkable story this is, for it shows how profound simple acts of kindness can have on other human beings.

When we look at kindness, here are just three things to consider:

First, kindness is a virtue, and a virtue is a positive trait or quality. Virtues are seen as habits, things that become part of us primarily through practice. The more we practice a virtue, the stronger and more firmly embedded it becomes in our innermost being. Oftentimes, we hear that as Christians, we are to clothe ourselves with a robe of virtue. This means that we are to be known as virtuous people. The opposite of virtue is, of course, vice or evil. So, a virtuous person is easily recognized by living a life characterized by goodness instead of evil.

Second, kindness is a virtue that we can practice anywhere, at any time, with anyone. We can practice kindness in our homes with spouses, children, brothers or sisters. When we are tempted to engage in evil actions, such as making a sarcastic remark or being selfish, we go in the opposite direction and say or do something kind. Practicing kindness can be a lot of fun, and sometimes people are so amazed at kindness, that they begin to act kind towards others. It can be contagious. Recently, I was in line at a grocery store, and the woman in front of me did not have enough coupons and money to buy a particular item. She told the clerk she'd have to skip buying the item. I said, "Oh, I'd be happy to buy that for you." The woman was astonished at my offer and, as luck would have it, the clerk recognized me and told the woman that I was the Pastor of St. Mary Catholic Church. The customer said, "I can't get over it! I'm going to tell all my friends! I just can't believe it."

And third, sometimes kindness can reap rewards for ourselves, just as unkindness can harm us. Currently, there is a program about how big hotels operate. When customers are nice to the people at the front desk, they tend to get marked as "good" customers and get nicer treatment. Likewise, troublemakers tend to get punished.

As we continue our life journeys this week, it would be a good idea to take a look at our own lives. How do we practice kindness in our lives? How do we fail at this at times?

And that is the good news I have for you on this Third Sunday in Advent.

Story Source: Schlatter, John Wayne. "A Simple Gesture." Web, 2012.

Chapter 4

4th Sunday of Advent - C
Disney's Secret of Life

Scripture:

- Micah 5: 1-4a
- Psalm 80: 2ac & 3b, 15-16, 18-19
- Hebrews 10: 5-10
- Luke 1: 39-45

Today, Catholic Christians celebrate the Fourth Sunday of Advent. In the Gospel of Luke, we hear the story of Mary traveling to the hill country to visit her relatives, Zachariah and Elizabeth. Mary had heard that Elizabeth was pregnant even though Elizabeth was over the usual child-bearing age.

When Elizabeth heard Mary's greeting, Elizabeth became filled with the Holy Spirit and said the words that Catholic Christians use in one of our prayers, the Hail Mary. Elizabeth said, "Blessed are you among women, and blessed is the fruit of your womb" (Luke 1: 42). Elizabeth went on to say that upon Mary's greeting, the infant in her womb "leaped for joy" (Luke 1: 44). The infant was, of course, the one we know today as "St. John the Baptist," the herald or announcer of Jesus' arrival.

We can only imagine what it must have been like for Mary and Elizabeth as they visited each other. Both were pregnant and filled with all the hopes and dreams and questions that any expectant parent might experience. Further, this was their first pregnancy each, so they had no firsthand knowledge about the usual course of pregnancy, birth and raising a child.

Because of their humanity, and because of their inexperience with the biological and social life processes unfolding in their lives, they were filled with wonder. And we, too, are filled with wonder all the time in our own lives. We frequently wonder what life is all about and if we are following God's plan for us. That is what the little boy in the following story wondered.

There was once an 8-year old boy who liked to think about life. One day, he approached an old man who was standing by a wishing well. The boy went up to the old man and said, "I understand that you are a very wise man. I'd like to know the secret of life."

The old man looked at the boy, smiled, and said, "I have thought about that very question much in my lifetime, and I think that the secret of life can be summed up in four words.

"The first is THINK. Think about the values by which you wish to live your life.

"The second is BELIEVE. Believe in yourself based on the thinking that you have done about the values that you are going to use to live your life.

"The third is DREAM. Dream about the things that you can be, based on your own belief in yourself and the values by which you're going to live your life.

"The fourth is DARE. Dare to make your dreams become reality, based on your belief in yourself and your values."

With that, Walt Disney, one of the most creative Americans of the Twentieth Century, said to the boy, "Think, Believe, Dream, and Dare."

The advice Walt Disney gave to the little boy was very solid. Not only can we point out these in the life of Mary, we each have what it takes to make them a reality in our own lives.

First, we think of the values we have. As Catholic Christians, we have been taught basic values or virtues in our homes and faith formation programs since we were infants. We know how we are supposed to live our lives and we know what virtues we are supposed to adopt and cultivate. Among the vast array of virtues are honesty, hard work, courage, generosity, humility, kindness, perseverance, joy and the like.

Second, we must believe in ourselves. We must believe that we have the ability to practice the virtues that we hold dear in our daily lives. There is absolutely no virtue that you and I are incapable of putting into practice. It is not always easy, of course, to be virtuous. Sometimes, we are tempted to abandon our virtues or values because of biological urges, peer pressure, greed, pride, anger, or whatever. But just because something is difficult does not mean we are incapable of putting them into practice.

Third, we need to dream. Dreaming is putting our minds into the future and imagining all the wonderful things we can do and can be. Just imagine all the dreaming Mary and Elizabeth did together as they envisioned being mothers and what they wanted for their yet-to-be-born children. Like all parents, I'm sure they wanted nothing but the very best for the children and they wanted to be the best mothers ever. And, please, never think that dreaming for the future is something only for the young.

And fourth, we need to dare. We need to live our values on a daily basis and we need to make our dreams a reality. This is called doing God's will. This is called doing hard work. This is called persevering in our vocation. If we do not dare to put our dreams into reality, our dreams are nothing but dreams. Dreams, no matter how noble, are like fog or puffs of smoke if they are not made concrete in our lives.

In summary, we must believe that we all have the basic values to lead a good life. We need to dream for the future and then make our dreams a reality. Then, we will have one of the most precious of all gifts - serenity or a sense of peacefulness in our spirits.

As we continue our life journeys this week, it would be a good idea to ask ourselves how we are putting our dreams into action.

And that is the good news I have for you on this Fourth Sunday of Advent.

Story Source: Anonymous. "The Secret of Life." *Sower's Seeds of Encouragement: Fifth Planting,* Ed. Brian Cavanaugh. NY: Paulist Press, 1998. #75, p. 71.

Chapter 5

Christmas - C
A Patch of Christmas

Scripture: (from Mass during the Night)

- Isaiah 9: 1-6
- Psalm 96: 1-2a, 2b-3, 11-12, 13
- Titus 2: 11-14
- Luke 2: 1-14

Christmas has finally arrived, and we gather to give thanks for all of our many blessings. On behalf of the staff and faculty and other ministers of St. Mary Parish, I wish you and those you love a very Merry Christmas! I pray that God will make all your Christmas dreams come true.

In today's reading from the Prophet Isaiah, we get a glimpse into how the people in ancient times imagined the Messiah would be. One idea they had was that when the Messiah, or Savior, came to Earth, he would be the "Prince of Peace" (Is 9:6) and that "...there shall be endless peace" (Is 9:7). And in the Gospel of St. Luke, we hear, "And suddenly there was a multitude of the heavenly host with the angel, praising God and saying: 'Glory to God in the highest and on earth peace to those on whom his favor rests'" (Luke 2: 13-14).

Now, when most of us hear the word "peace," we think of the absence of war. This is, of course, one meaning of the word. But in Catholic Christianity, "peace" means ordered tranquility that comes from the right relationship between ourselves and God and our neighbors. In other words, to live "in peace" means that we live our lives in harmony with what we believe God wants from us, and we treat all other human beings as though they were Jesus Himself. So, when we say that Jesus is the Prince of Peace, we mean that He came to show us how we are to relate to God and to each other.

In the United States, there is no time of the year when people are more inclined to follow the meaning of peace and goodwill than Christmastime. Even the hardest of hearts are often softened by the magic of the season and generosity and joy flourish from unexpected sources in unexpected ways.

But Americans do not have a monopoly on the magic of Christmas. It can be seen in other times and by other people of the world. That is exactly what we see in the following story that occurred in Europe during World War I.

It was a cold Christmas Eve, and a group of English soldiers were snuggled in their trenches. In front of the trenches was something called "No Man's Land," a piece of land where conflict between soldiers would not occur. On the other side of No Man's Land, German soldiers were snuggled in their own trenches.

A teenage English soldier whom I'll call Ethan softly said to himself, "It's rotten to be here on Christmas Eve."

The older soldier next to him, agreed. He said, "If I were back home in England, I'd be sitting in front of a toasty fireplace and not in this cold, muddy trench. I'd be eating a delicious Christmas dinner and singing Christmas carols with my family, and afterwards I'd be bouncing my little boy and girl on my knees. Oh, I don't want to think about it. It just makes it more miserable to be here."

"I suppose you're right," Ethan replied. Both men once again retreated into their silent thoughts of home.

Suddenly, from far down the trench, the men heard an English soldier singing, "Silent Night." Soon, other voices chimed in. Soon, the English soldiers began to hear "Silent Night" in German from across No Man's Land. Soon, both the German and English soldiers were singing this beautiful song of Christmas peace in their own language.

No one knows what prompted him, but throwing caution to the wind, Ethan got out of the trench, threw down his rifle, and began walking across No Man's Land. Then, a German soldier got out of his trench, threw his rifle down, and began walking towards Ethan. The example of two young soldiers was contagious, and soon all of the soldiers were doing the same. They began shaking hands and sharing the food and gifts they had with each other. They showed each other photos of their wives or girlfriends and children back home in England or Germany. They even cut down some little trees and brought them into No Man's Land and decorated them and sang Christmas carols together. They even played a soccer game right in the middle of No Man's Land.

For a short while, a patch of Christmas was seen on earth in a warzone. Soldiers sang about peace on Earth, and they threw down their guns. There was indeed peace on Earth in this little corner of God's universe.

Now, a century later, we are celebrating Christmas. And we see a world where many people don't always treat each other with dignity and respect.

But you and I have a choice. Just like the German and English soldiers of long ago came together to create a special patch of Christmas in a dismal place, we can and should create a patch of Christmas everywhere we travel on our life journeys. What a wonderful world this would be if we could just remember that and create the magic of Christmas.

And that is the good news I have for you on this Christmas.

Story Source: Goodhue, Thomas W. "Story for Christmas." *Sharing the Good News with Children: Stories for the Common Lectionary*. Cincinnati, OH: St. Anthony Messenger Press, 1992. pp. 21-23.

An earlier version can be found in the Upper Room's *Pockets*, December, 1982.

Chapter 6

The Holy Family of Jesus, Mary and Joseph - C
Detachment and Two Monks

Scripture:

- 1 Samuel 1: 20-22, 24-28
- Psalm 84: 2-3, 5-6, 9-10
- 1 John 3: 1-2, 21-24
- Luke 2: 41-52

Today, Catholic Christians celebrate the feast of the Holy Family—Jesus, Mary, and Joseph.

On this day, we hear a very interesting but strange story in the Gospel of Luke about the Holy Family going to Jerusalem for Passover celebrations. When the festival was completed, Mary and Joseph, along with their family and friends, began traveling back home. During the first day's journey home, Mary and Joseph thought that Jesus was with some of their friends or acquaintances somewhere in the caravan. However, when they went to look for him at the end of the day, he was nowhere to be found.

Alarmed, Joseph and Mary went back to Jerusalem to find Jesus. They searched for three days before finding him in the temple talking with the religious teachers. The Scripture says that the leaders were astonished at his understanding.

When Mary told Jesus how worried she and Joseph had been, Jesus simply replied, "Why were you looking for me? Did you not know that I must be in my Father's house?" Jesus did, however, leave the temple and go back home with Joseph and Mary and was obedient to them.

This is a very strange story in so many ways, and it identifies many themes of everyday life. For example, what did Jesus eat for three days? Where did he sleep? Didn't he think his folks would be worried about him?

In the story, we see a common fear that all parents have - that of losing a child. We also catch a glimpse into the very difficult stage of life between childhood and adulthood.

There is another very important theme present in this story, however, that is critical for all of us on our spiritual journey—detachment.

Detachment in the spiritual life refers to becoming free from whatever obstacles we may have in following God's plan for us. Some of these obstacles are people, places, and things. At times, they can also be thoughts as we see in the following story.

Once, there were two monks walking silently on a path enjoying the beauty of nature all around them. When they got to a river, they met a beautiful woman who appeared to be in great distress. She told them that despite many attempts, she had been unable to cross the swiftly-flowing river by herself. The stronger of the two monks told her not to worry. He then picked her up in his arms and carried her across the river and put her down gently on the opposite shore. He accepted her thanks, and she continued her journey in one direction, while the two monks continued their journey in another direction.

The two monks walked on in silence for a couple of hours. Suddenly, the monk who had not carried the woman began to berate his fellow monk. He said, "You know we are celibates, and we have taken a sacred vow never to entertain impure thoughts of a woman. Yet, you knowingly held a beautiful woman in your arms close to you, holding her as though your two bodies were one as you slowly crossed the river. It's a shocking violation of our vows of chastity!"

The monk who had carried the woman listened carefully to the criticism and examined his own actions. "You're right," he responded. "We did take vows, and I did pick up the woman in my arms, and I did carry her across the river. But I did do it with pure intentions. However, I set her down on the shore. However, you, my dear brother, are still carrying her in your head!"

This is a wonderful story because it illustrates that we can allow even thoughts to serve as obstacles on our spiritual journeys.

Three other common obstacles that can block our detachment are people, places, and things.

First, some people are so attached to people that they cannot live out their adult vocations. I knew a young man once who believed he had a vocation to be a Religious Brother. He loved to talk about how wonderful that life would be, but he had one big argument against actually leaving his home and entering a Religious community: he had to care for his parents. As it turned out, his parents were fine and fully functional. The young man argued, however, that they were "getting older" and one day might need him. When I pointed out that every person's parents are getting older and one day will die, he began to see the folly of this attachment. Today, he is a Religious Brother.

Second, places can capture us. Because I have spent so much of my life in university towns, I have seen many people fall so much in love with such towns and never leave. Often in university towns you will find people with master's degrees driving taxicabs or working in retail stores instead of moving on to work in the fields for which they were prepared but which are located in distant cities.

And third, some people are so attached to their immovable possessions that they cannot part with them. Now I believe homes are wonderful, but only if that is where you are flourishing and joyful. If you are "stuck" in a place because you simply can't afford to move, that is very problematic for your spiritual life.

As we continue our life journeys this week, it would be a good idea to reflect on our own detachment. Are there things in our lives that we can't let go to follow the Lord more fully?

And that is the good news I have for you on this Feast of the Holy Family.

Story Source: "Two monks traveling" by Anonymous. In Brian Cavanaugh's *More Sower's Seeds: Second Planting*, New York: Paulist Press, 1992, #20, pp. 22-23.

Chapter 7

Epiphany - C
The Star

Scripture:

- Isaiah 60: 1-6
- Psalm 72: 1-2, 7-8, 10-11, 12-13
- Ephesians 3: 2-3a, 5-6
- Matthew 2: 1-12

Today, Catholic Christians celebrate the very ancient Feast of the Epiphany, sometimes called "Little Christmas" or the "Feast of the Three Kings." In the Western branch of the Catholic Church, of which we are part, this Feast commemorates the showing of the Christ Child to the visitors from the East. The great news of this Feast for us is that Jesus came for all people, not just for the Jews.

This Feast has many symbols. Sometimes the Feast is symbolized by three crowns of the wise men. Other times, it is symbolized by the gifts of gold, frankincense, and myrrh representing Christ's divinity, his priesthood, and his eventual death on the cross. And, finally, the feast is symbolized by the star that led the visitors from the East to the Messiah.

In this homily, we focus on the symbol of the star. Symbols, as you know, are words or objects that stand for something else. A heart, for example, is a common symbol of love, just as a shamrock is a symbol of the Blessed Trinity. Stars are common symbols in flags of nations (such as the United States) and of religions.

In the following story, we see how one young person saw the star as a symbol of leadership - the type of leadership to which you and I and all Christians are called by virtue of our baptism.

There was once a little girl named Kaitlinn who was very excited about being in the annual Christmas pageant. She had told her family that she had the main part in the play, so they assumed that she must be playing the part of the Virgin Mary.

On the evening of the play, Kaitlinn's parents and other relatives joined the others in the audience. Kaitlinn sat quietly and confidently at the edge of the stage.

Suddenly, the teacher began, "A long time ago, Mary and Joseph had a baby and then they named him Jesus. And when Jesus was born, a bright star appeared in the sky over the stable where he was born."

At that cue, Kaitlinn got up, picked up a long pole which had a large, glittering star attached to the end of it by a string. She walked behind Mary and Joseph and held the star up high so everyone could see.

When the teacher told about how the shepherds came to see the Baby Jesus, Kaitlinn jiggled her pole so that the glimmering star danced around. Then, when the Three Wise Men responded to their cue, Kaitlinn went towards them and led them to the Baby Jesus. Little Kaitlinn's face radiated with joy.

After the play ended and everyone had enjoyed refreshments, Kaitlinn and her family went home. On the way home, Kaitlinn said, "I had the main part in the play."

"You did?" asked one of her family members.

"Yes, because I showed everybody how to find Jesus."

Now most of us would have said that Jesus, Mary, and Joseph held the main parts of the play. But for little Kaitlinn, the star had the best role, for it was the light that showed people how to get to the Christ Child. And the more we think about it, the wiser little Kaitlinn becomes.

Each of us, by virtue of our baptism, is a priest. At our baptism, the Holy Spirit entered into each of us with many gifts, and we were made part of what is called the "priesthood of all believers." As Christians and priests, we are called to be lights to the world and lamps in the darkness. We are to be shining examples to the rest of the world to show them how a person who is reborn in Christ Jesus lives. We serve as lamps by being living, walking homilies. Anyone who observes us from afar should be able to say, "That person is living their life as a Christian."

But how, exactly, do we go about being a light to the world? I submit that we do it in three ways: through our thoughts, words, and deeds.

First, we mentally remember that we are Christians and members of Christ's royal priesthood. That means we are to continually take a moral inventory of ourselves. We do this by thinking before acting, for example, or when we examine our consciences at the end of the day to see what we did well and what we did not do well.

Second, we do this through our words. When I talk about being a light to the world by our words, I'm not necessarily referring to preaching about Jesus. Rather, I'm referring to the type of language we use. I believe that priests should avoid using bad language, not because it is necessarily sinful, but because as followers of Christ, they should be above such things. And because every baptized person is a priest, that applies to all of us. Though using foul, vulgar, or obscene language is not sinful for most people, it is still not something one should expect from an "alter Christos" or "another Christ" which is what priests are.

And third, we are lights to the world by our deeds. In modern day America, we often hear people say, "You need to walk the walk, not just talk the talk." Talk is cheap. Anybody can say good things. But putting our good intentions into action is what people are attracted to. Do we claim generosity is a virtue? Fine, then show it. Do we claim forgiveness is a virtue? Fine, then show it.

As we continue our life journeys this week, it would be good idea to take a look at our own lives. How are we being lights to the world? How are our thoughts, words, and deeds reflecting our own priesthood that we were given at our baptism?

That is the good news I have for you on this Feast of the Epiphany.

Story Source: Anonymous. "The Star." *Sower's Seeds Aplenty: Fourth Planting*, Ed. Brian Cavanaugh. NY: Paulist Press, 1996. #74, pp. 56-57.

Chapter 8

Baptism of Jesus - C
Temperance & the Poor Man

Scripture:

- Isaiah 40: 1-5, 9-11
- Psalm 104: 1b-2, 3-4, 24-25, 27-28, 29-30
- Titus 2: 11-14; 3: 4-7
- Luke 3: 15-16, 21-22

Today, Catholic Christians celebrate the Baptism of Jesus by his cousin, John the Baptist, in the Jordan River. Though Jesus had no need of baptism, he availed himself of this Jewish ritual so that the Holy Spirit could come down and God the Father proclaim that Jesus was, indeed, his beloved son.

In addition to hearing the baptism story of Jesus, we also hear some ideas that St. Paul had on how to be a good Christian in his Letter to Titus. In this letter, Paul tells Titus, who was head of the Church on the Island of Crete, to give some instruction to his Christians on how to behave. In today's selection from the Letter of Titus, Paul says that Christians should "...reject godless ways and worldly desires and to live temperately, justly, and devoutly..." (Titus 2: 12).

Today, we look at the concept of "temperance." Although temperance has been used to mean total abstinence from drinking alcohol, in today's context, it refers to living life with moderation and self-restraint. In Catholic Christian thought, temperance is one of the four cardinal or hinge virtues, the others being prudence, fortitude and justice. Temperance allows people to live balanced lives.

Temperance, like all virtues, is a habit, and habits must be practiced to become strong and embedded in our spirits. Just because we consider virtues to be good does not necessarily mean that they are always easy to put into practice. That is what we see in the following story that is based on a folktale from the Brothers Grimm.

There was once a very poor man who was always complaining that the world was unfair. He would often say to anyone who would listen that "Most of those who are rich did nothing to deserve their wealth. They inherited their money from their parents."

One day, as the poor man was walking home from expressing his bitter feelings to a crowd in the town square, Fortune appeared to him. Fortune said, "I have decided to provide you with wealth. All you have to do is to hold out your purse, and I will fill it with gold coins. There is one condition, however, that you must remember. If any of the coins fall out of the purse onto the ground, everything I gave you will become dust. Be very careful, because I see that your purse is very old; do not overload it."

The poor man was overwhelmed with joy at his newfound fortune. He opened the strings of his purse and watched as Fortune began to pour a stream of golden coins into it. The purse soon became very heavy.

Fortune asked, "Is that enough?"

"Not yet," cried the poor man.

Fortune poured in several more gold coins, so that the purse was filled. "Shall I stop?" asked Fortune.

"Not yet," replied the poor man. "Add just a few more."

But at that moment, the purse split apart, and the gold coins fell to the ground, and the treasure turned into dust. Fortune disappeared, and the man was left with an empty purse.

Needless to say, the poor man was crushed. It is said that he never forgave himself for being so greedy, for his greed caused him to lose all.

This is a very interesting story for us, for it shows that temperance is not always easy to achieve. The virtue of temperance, which calls us to be moderate in using the things of this world and to exercise self-restraint, can elude us. There are so many temptations around us that we can often behave in very non-temperate ways. And, I think that of all the people on the planet, none are more in danger of being intemperate than Americans, for we have so many wonderful things at our fingertips. Let us look at three common things that can lead us to be intemperate in our daily lives:

First, American culture is geared to foster excess. We are always searching for bigger, better, faster, sleeker, more powerful things. If one is good, two is twice as good, three is three times as good, and so on. I am always amazed, for example, at how people on the Home & Garden Channel react to seeing master bedrooms and bathrooms for the first time when looking for a new home. Some of the bedrooms and bathrooms are absolutely huge, but the people dismiss them as being "too small." I often wonder exactly what they need so much space for in these two locations.

Second, impulse buying is too easy for us. We can be sitting in our easy chair watching television, for example, and a commercial comes on advertising a device that can make four pancakes at a time. And, the pancakes don't stick. It's wonderful! Just call the number on the screen, and if you're one of the first one hundred callers, the company will double your order! Such a great deal! So you reach into your pocket, take out your cell phone, call the number, and give your credit card information. Your order is complete. Never mind, of course, that you never prepare or eat pancakes; this is too good a deal to pass up!

And third, sometimes we get ourselves trapped by collections. We see something we like, such as an Oldies-But-Goodies collection, on television. We hear songs that take us down Memory Lane. It's only $14.95 for an album with wonderful oldies. What we fail to think through, though, is the collection is for twenty albums, so the actual cost by the time we're done is almost three hundred dollars, not counting outrageous "shipping and handling" fees.

As we continue our life journeys this week, it would be a good idea to examine our lives. How do we practice the virtue of temperance? What traps do we encounter that lead us to excesses?

And that is the good news I have for you on this Feast of the Baptism of Jesus.

Story Source: Anonymous. "Fortune and the Poor Man." *Stories for Telling: A Treasury for Christian Storytellers*, Ed. William R. White. Minneapolis: Augsburg Books, 1986. p. 111.

Part 2

LENT &
EASTER SEASONS

Chapter 9

1ˢᵗ Sunday of Lent - C
Socrates & Self-Knowledge

Scripture:

- Deuteronomy 26: 4-10
- Psalm 91: 1-2, 10-11, 12-13, 14-15
- Romans 10: 8-13
- Luke 4: 1-13

Today, Catholic Christians celebrate the First Sunday of Lent, the season of the year that goes from Ash Wednesday until the beginning of the Mass of the Lord's Supper on Holy Thursday.

During Lent, we prepare catechumens (that is, non-baptized persons) to receive Baptism at the Easter Vigil Mass. Also during Lent, baptized persons prepare themselves to renew their Baptism promises at Easter. To prepare ourselves, we examine our spiritual lives and attempt to strengthen them by giving up something pleasurable or by adding something good. In either case, the purpose is to show that the spirit is stronger than the flesh.

But whether we try giving up something like candy or television during Lent, or whether we try to add something to our spiritual lives such as saying a daily rosary, we will be tempted not to follow through on our intentions. And temptation is the subject of today's Gospel reading from St. Luke.

In Luke's story, Jesus is tempted by the devil. The devil tries to tempt Jesus with food and power and glory. But Jesus, being God, does not give into the temptations. Jesus knows how to fight temptation because he knows himself and human nature. And like Jesus, we too must know ourselves to be strong in our spiritual lives.

Catholic Christians are encouraged from the time we are small children to continually examine our lives. We are encouraged to conduct what is known as an "examination of conscience." In this exercise, we look at our daily lives to find the things we do well and the things we do poorly. The object of this exercise is to get rid of the weeds in our spiritual gardens and nurture the flowers or virtues that are growing.

Jesus, of course, encouraged people to look closely not only at their behaviors, but also at their inner selves. He challenged them to look at their motives. But Jesus' teaching, like that of other great teachers of the world, did not arise in a vacuum. On the contrary, the knowledge of great minds was handed down to them by other great teachers. One man who influenced our Church lived four centuries before Jesus, a man named Socrates.

Socrates was a Greek philosopher who taught through questioning. He believed that answers to basic truths were already inside us. If we are asked the right questions, we would eventually discover the truths ourselves. One of his greatest students was Plato, a man who had a profound influence on the early Catholic Church.

Although Socrates was noted for being disheveled and not very handsome, inside he had great beauty. Socrates could not believe, for example, that anyone would deliberately do wrong if they knew what was right. He had a very positive view of human nature, and he believed that knowledge and moral virtue were one and the same. If you were not virtuous, you didn't know much.

Today, however, we remember two very important things Socrates said that tie in completely with the Catholic view of the spiritual life. He said, "Know thyself" and, "An unexamined life is not worth living." These sayings tie into our discussion today, for if we do not know ourselves and examine what we are all about, we cannot grow spiritually.

When discussing temptation, each one of us needs to know that there will always be certain people, places and things that will lead us into temptation. And the best course of action is to avoid temptation whenever possible, for that is much easier than fighting temptation head-on.

First, there are certain people who seem to bring out the worst in us. Some people, for example, might love to gossip. And, because their gossip topics are so delicious, we find that it is almost impossible to break ourselves away from them. Other people make us angry or jealous. Some have a very negative view of the world, and being around them brings us down and makes us sad. Others make us angry because they are lazy or never on time or fail to show up when they say they will.

Second, there are certain places we should avoid if we know what is good for us. Recovering alcoholics, for example, almost never have a good reason for going into bars. That is why Alcoholics Anonymous groups don't meet in bars. Likewise, a credit card junkie should avoid cruising malls with a credit card in their pocket, just like someone on a weight-reducing diet should not be hanging around in donut shops, pizza parlors and candy shops.

And third, certain things may get us into trouble, so we should avoid them if at all possible. Perhaps we find that we get into trouble in Internet chat rooms. Or maybe we get into trouble with certain substances such as drugs.

Only by truly knowing ourselves can we firmly avoid people, places and things that tend to lead us into temptation. What may be trouble for one person may be no trouble at all for another.

As we continue our life journeys this week, it would be a good idea to take some time to do a good examination of conscience. What are the people, places and things that tempt me to do bad things or that harm my spiritual life? Which of them can I avoid, and which do I need to fight head-on?

And that is the good news I have for you on this First Sunday of Lent.

Chapter 10

2nd Sunday of Lent - C
Fr. Tony & Forgiveness

Scripture:

- Genesis 15: 5-12, 17-18
- Psalm 27: 1, 7-8, 9abc, 13-14
- Philippians 3: 17 - 4: 1
- Luke 9: 28b-36

Today, Catholic Christians celebrate the Second Sunday of Lent. On this Sunday, we hear the amazing story of the Transfiguration of Jesus. In this story, which has baffled Bible scholars for centuries, Jesus is with Peter, James, and John on a hill. As Jesus was praying, his face changed in appearance and his clothes became dazzling white. Suddenly, there were two men talking with him, Moses and Elijah. In the Old Testament world, Moses represents the Law, and Elijah represents the Prophets.

Peter, James and John had been asleep. When they awoke, they were astonished to see the scene before them. Immediately they thought of making three tents for Jesus, Moses and Elijah. Suddenly, though, a voice came from a cloud and said, "This is my chosen Son. Listen to him." After the voice had spoken, Moses and Elijah were no longer seen.

This story has been interpreted in many ways. For example, it shows with the coming of Jesus, He is all we need, for the Old Testament has now been fulfilled. That message is signified not only by the disappearance of Moses and Elijah, but by God the Father (the voice from the cloud) telling us that Jesus is His Son and to listen to Him.

When we hear such stories as the Transfiguration, we are challenged to make sense of it in our own lives. I believe that just as the non-sparkling Jesus showed his humanity, the dazzling white garments showed his divinity. He is both God and human. As Christians, we are to imitate Christ. It's easy to see how we can imitate the human Jesus because we're human. The question is, though, how can we imitate Jesus the God?

Many Catholic Christian writers, like writers in other religious traditions, have held that in every human being, there is something called the "divine spark." In other words, we humans reflect our Creator in a way that other creatures do not. Thus, we are to reflect God in our actions. Sometimes, however, we forget that we possess a divine spark. Sometimes we forget that God is our Father and loves us beyond words. And in those times we forget, we need a reminder. That is what happened to a man in the story of Fr. Tony as told by Fr. William J. Bausch.

Fr. Tony Williams had been a missionary in the African nation of Tanzania for about 17 years. He eventually developed abdominal cancer and had surgery for it. After a period of recuperation, he went back to his work. Fr. Tony was a very personable man whom the people loved deeply.

He was gracious and kind, and he had a great sense of humor that made people laugh.

After his missionary assignment was up, Fr. Tony returned to the United States. Unfortunately, after a few years back in the country, his cancer came back, and he learned that he only had a short time to live. He lived at the headquarters of his religious community, and different people would come to visit him regularly.

One day, Fr. Tony asked to have the superior general of the Order to come and visit him. He told the superior general about an experience he had had the night before. Fr. Tony reported that as he was lying in his bed trying to pray. He was gazing on the face of the crucified Christ in a picture. Suddenly, the eyes of Christ began to shine and look at him. Then, Fr. Tony was drawn into the picture and arrived on Calvary precisely at the time when Jesus was being crucified and the soldiers were hammering nails into Jesus' hands.

Suddenly, Fr. Tony saw the face of one of the soldiers, and it was his own face. He was horrified. Fr. Tony asked Jesus, "Have I been that terrible? After all, I've led a comparatively good and decent life. I really haven't done anything that horrible. Is it possible that my sins are crucifying you? Are they that evil and bad?" Jesus smiled kindly at Fr. Tony and said, "Tony, whatever they are, your sins are forgiven. My peace I give to you."

After hearing Jesus' words, the face of the soldier disappeared and Fr. Tony came out of the experience. He said that ever since then, he had experienced enormous peace that Jesus spoke of in the gospel.

Now as time went on, and it became clear that Fr. Tony's days on earth were coming to an end, many members of his very large family came to visit. Everyone reported the same thing: That the minute they entered the room, an incredible sense of peace engulfed them.

In his final minutes alive, Fr. Tony told people that his one wish for them was that they could have the same peace he had received – the peace that comes from knowing that Jesus died for our sins and loves us. After telling his visitors that, he died with a big smile on his face.

This beautiful story shows the divine spark that spiritual writers have identified. Fr. Tony was transfigured or transformed from the physical realm of suffering to a higher realm. I have heard from many people through the years who have had cancer and other forms of physical and mental illness. Though they usually fought for the life of the body and mind, they reported that it was serenity, or the sense of spiritual peace, that truly brought them joy. Everything else was not so important.

As we continue our life journey this week, it would be a good idea to reflect on our own lives. How does the divine spark show itself in our lives? How do we seek to learn from those suffering from physical and mental illnesses?

And that is the good news I have for you on this Second Sunday of Lent.

Story Source: Anonymous. "Fr. Tony." *A World of Stories for Preachers and Teachers*, Ed. William J. Bausch. 1998, #57, pp. 183-184.

Chapter 11

3rd Sunday of Lent - C
Daniel Bears Fruit

Scripture:

- Exodus 3: 1-8a, 13-15
- Psalm 103: 1-2, 3-4, 6-7, 8 & 11
- 1 Corinthians 10: 1-6, 10-12
- Luke 13: 1-9

Today, Catholic Christians celebrate the Third Sunday of Lent. On this Sunday, we hear the interesting parable of Jesus about the fig tree that grew in a garden. One day, the owner of the garden came up to the fig tree and noticed that it was not producing any fruit. As a result, he gave the order to the gardener to cut the tree down because it was the third year in a row that the tree had failed to produce fruit. The gardener, however, pleaded for the tree's life. He said he would work with the tree and nurture it so that it would bear fruit in the future.

In this story, the fig tree represents us, and the owner of the garden is God the Father. Jesus is, of course, the gardener who loves each and every one of us. Jesus is always intervening to give us another chance – to help us to produce fruit. It is Jesus who wants to help us in every way so that we can be all that we can be.

Frequently, people do grow and bear fruit, but they fail to realize this. They begin to confuse human action with earthly results. That is what happened to a young man I'll call Daniel.

Daniel was a man in his middle 20s who earned a bachelor's degree in business. After college, he got a job near his home in North Carolina. Though he was able to do his work, he was afflicted with the disease of alcoholism which ran in his family.

As time went on, Daniel began to suffer in many life realms. For example, he began to notice that his mental health was affected by periods of depression, remorse and feelings of guilt. He lacked joy in his life. His spirituality also suffered as he began to engage in behaviors that were not in harmony with his value system. All of his leisure time was alcohol-centered, and he noticed that he could not remember the next day what he had said or did at parties the night before.

Daniel also began to suffer financial strain as a result of impulse-spending while drinking, and he frequently found himself engaging in risky behaviors while on dates. Friends began to shy away from him, and he began to isolate himself.

Fortunately for Daniel, however, his boss was a recovering alcoholic himself and recognized the symptoms of alcoholism in Daniel. As a result, he invited Daniel to go to an Alcoholics Anonymous meeting with him. Daniel agreed. Daniel was one of the lucky alcoholics who recognized his disease immediately when he heard the stories of the speakers at the meeting.

Daniel continued to go to A.A. meetings and to follow the program. Soon, he began to see definite changes in his mental health, spirituality, finances and other life realms.

When he felt comfortable in his sobriety, he began dating a nurse from a local hospital, and he was extremely fulfilled. In fact, after several months of dating, he was thinking of asking her to marry him. The woman, however, decided that she did not want to get married, and she broke off the relationship.

Devastated, Daniel decided to take a job in California that he had heard about. He felt that a change of location would be good for him.

Daniel loved his new job, and he found he did not miss North Carolina. Though he still thought of the young woman whom he had given his heart to, he came to the realization that it was for the best. After all, he reasoned, it is better to get out of a relationship than get out of a marriage.

In his new life, Daniel continued to be active in Alcoholics Anonymous. In fact, he served as a sponsor for many newcomers to the program. He became active in his local parish, St. Barbara, and joined their prison ministry and served as a lector at weekend Masses. He also helped the poor and elderly do their tax forms at tax time.

Soon, however, Daniel lost his job because the company decided to outsource his job overseas where salaries were much lower.

Daniel began to sink into depression once again, but he was smart enough to not start drinking. He began to see himself as a failure. He began to think he was like the fig tree that produced no fruit. He began to think God must be displeased with him.

Fortunately, however, Daniel had a priest who took an interest in him. The priest told Daniel that God judges us on our behavior, not on the results of our behavior. The priest gave Daniel an example of making amends. He said, "Daniel, if you harm someone, it is good for you to say 'I'm sorry.' If the other person accepts it, that's fine. If they reject it, that's fine. The important thing is that you said 'I'm sorry.' That is the fruit God is looking for." The priest gave Daniel another example. He said, "Giving a homeless, hungry person some money for food is good fruit. What the person does with the money has nothing to do with your generosity."

Once Daniel began to realize that his actions, rather than how others were responding to his actions, were the "fruit" of the Christian, he began to realize that God was judging him on the things in life he could control or change, not on things that were outside of his control or ability to change. For the first time, Daniel began to truly appreciate the beginning of the Serenity Prayer: "God grant me the serenity to accept the things I cannot change, courage to change the things I can, and the wisdom to know the difference."

What kinds of fruits do we produce in our lives? How does Jesus work with us to be Christ-like in our actions?

And that is the good news I have for you on this Third Sunday of Lent.

Chapter 12

4th Sunday of Lent - C
Grudges & Forgiveness

Scripture:

- Joshua 5: 9a, 10-12
- Psalm 34: 2-3, 4-5, 6-7
- 2 Corinthians 5: 17-21
- Luke 15: 1-3, 11-32

Today, Catholic Christians celebrate the Fourth Sunday of Lent. On this day, we hear the beautiful parable of the Prodigal Son.

In this story, the younger of two sons asks for his inheritance. After receiving it, he leaves his father's house and lives a wild and reckless lifestyle. Finally, after his money runs out, he finds himself in despair. He decides to go home and beg his father to take him in as a servant. The father, however, upon seeing his son come up the road, is overwhelmed with joy. The father forgives his son even before the son opens his mouth.

In this story, the father represents God and God's total love for each of us. He is always ready to forgive us, and his love is everlasting. Nothing we can ever do can destroy his love for us, because God is love.

This story also shows resentment that the older son, who never left home, feels towards his wayward brother who is getting all the attention. The father reassures him, however, that everything the father owns belongs to the elder son. He wants the elder son to rejoice with him, for the younger son was lost and now is found. We can only hope that the older son does, indeed, rejoice, for the lack of forgiveness can cause great harm to one's wellbeing. That is what we see in the amazing story of a man from Milwaukee, Wisconsin named Matthew. The story, found on Cracked.Com, is by Xavier Jackson & Chris Radomile.

Matthew seemed to be an ordinary person. But what people around him did not know, was that Matthew was harboring grudges. Instead of letting go of the hurts of the past, he never forgot and never forgave. Then, one day in 2003, Matthew "snapped," he totally lost control of himself and decided to pay back some of the people on his grudge list.

First, he grabbed a can of fluorescent spray paint and covered the house of the first person on his grudge list. He painted obscenities, threats, and taunts. The reason he did this to the residence of the 75-year-old man who lived in the house was that he blamed this man for getting him fired from a low-paying job at a grocery store 10 years earlier. Yes, you heard correctly, 10 years earlier!

Matthew then went to the house of a man who had intervened in a fight Matthew had had with a girl in a parking lot five years earlier. Matthew not only spray-painted the house of this man, he dumped all of the man's potted plants into his hot tub. Before leaving the property, however, Matthew slashed a couple of the man's tires.

At the third house, Matthew apparently ran out of spray paint. Instead, he dumped paint stripper all over the cars that were parked at or around the house. The reason he did this at the third house was because he believed that the woman who lived in the house had cut him off in traffic.

This true story reminds us of the power that grudges can have in a human life and the evil they can produce. Fortunately, though, grudges can be eliminated in our lives.

Grudges refer to holding ill-will or resentments toward other persons for something they did to us in the past. One of the most powerful quotes about grudges comes from a writer named Anne Lamott who said, "Not forgiving is like drinking rat poison and then waiting for the rat to die." They are stupid because they do not harm the person we have ill-feelings about. On the contrary, they only hurt us.

In the Gospels, Jesus frequently gives each of us the commandment to forgive those who harm us. Thus, when we fail to forgive, we violate this Christian commandment. But failing to forgive others, or holding grudges, also harms our health.

The staff of the famous Mayo Clinic wrote a piece on grudges and how dangerous they are to us. The staff noted that when we carry around feelings of anger, bitterness, or vengeance, we can suffer in many life realms. For example, grudges can lead to anxiety and depression in our lives. They can also lead one to abuse material substances such as alcohol and other drugs, money, food and the like.

The good news, though, is that forgiving others can lead to better mental and spiritual health. It can lead to lower blood pressure and fewer symptoms of depression and anxiety. It can decrease our chances of abusing substances. And because it helps our spiritual and mental health, it can lead to better all-around physical health.

Forgiveness does not mean forgetting. Forgiveness is an act of the will, while forgetting things is a biochemical reaction. When we forgive, we are making the conscious choice to become free of resentments or grudges. We realize resentments only hurt us, not the person about whom we are angry. Forgiveness does not mean we necessarily condone the act the person did to hurt us, and forgiveness does not mean we necessarily "like" the person who hurt us. Forgiveness does mean, however, that we will not behave on the basis of grudges. For example, it means we will not bring up the unpleasant incident to others, and it means we will treat that person with respect even if not with warm friendliness.

As we continue our life journey this week, it would be a good idea to examine our lives. Do we carry around any grudges? Do we need to forgive others so that we can achieve the best mental, physical and spiritual health possible?

And that is the good news I have for you on this Fourth Sunday of Lent.

Story Source: Story of Matthew Mundschau is from "5 people who held grudges well past the point of sanity" on Cracked.Com by Xavier Jackson & Chris Radomile, April 21, 2012.

Chapter 13

5th Sunday of Lent - C
Judgment & the Mango Tree

Scripture:

- Isaiah 43: 16-21
- Psalm 126: 1-2ab, 2cd-3, 4-5, 6
- Philippians 3: 8-14
- John 8: 1-11

Today, Catholic Christians celebrate the Fifth Sunday of Lent, which means that Holy Week is just one week away.

On this day, we hear the interesting story of the woman caught in adultery. The Pharisees brought the woman to Jesus. They reminded Jesus that according to Mosaic Law, such a woman should be stoned to death. The Pharisees then asked Jesus what he thought about the case.

Jesus bent down and began to write something in the sand with his finger. He then said, "Let the one among you who is without sin be the first to throw a stone at her." He then began to write again in the sand. Although there is no mention in the Scriptures about what Jesus wrote in the sand, Bible scholars believe that perhaps it was the sins of Pharisees. They come to this conclusion because one by one, the Pharisees went away and left the woman standing alone with Jesus.

When there was no one left to accuse her, Jesus told the woman he would not condemn her either. He told her to go and sin no more.

The phrase "Let the one who is without sin throw the first stone" is so famous that pretty much everyone uses it from time to time. It means that we should not judge others, for we, too, are sinners. Furthermore, we do not know the life journeys of others. We do not know what struggles they have gone through and are going through, nor do we know how they have changed from one point in their life to another.

In the following ancient story called "Judgment in All Its Seasons," we see how four sons learned this lesson very well.

There was once a Persian king who wanted to teach his sons not to make rash judgments about people. Therefore, he commanded his eldest son to make a journey in winter to see a mango tree across the valley. When spring came, the king sent the next oldest son to visit the same tree. When summer arrived, the next-to-the-youngest son went to see this mango tree. Finally, in the autumn, the youngest son visited this same tree.

The king gathered all his sons after the youngest son had returned from his journey, and he asked each son to give a report on the mango tree. The first son, who had visited the tree in winter, said that the tree looked like an old stump. The second son, who had visited in springtime, said the tree was lovely to look at, large and green. The third son, who had visited in summer, reported that the tree had blossoms as beautiful as roses. The fourth son, who had just returned from his autumn journey, said that his brothers were all wrong. To him it was a tree filled with luscious, juicy fruit, like pears.

The wise king smiled at his sons and said, "Well, each one of you is correct." Seeing the puzzled look in their eyes, the king said, "You see, each of you saw the mango tree in a different season, thus you all correctly described what you saw. The lesson," said the king, "is to withhold judgment until you have seen the tree in all its seasons."

In the story of Jesus and the woman caught in adultery, and in this ancient fable of the king and his sons, we are reminded of the danger of judgmentalism or judging others. Judgmentalism refers to an eagerness to find fault with other people, coupled with a slowness to find fault with one's self. According to Author Jerry Bridges, judgementalism is one of the so-called "respectable sins" – sins that we tolerate on a regular basis.

Judgmentalism is wrong for many reasons. First, it is a sin against the Christian commandment: "Judge not lest you be judged" (Matthew 7:1). Many Christians are easily able to rattle off the Jewish Ten Commandments, but because the Christian Commandments were not put in a nice little package on a rock, they are ignorant of them. It is against Jesus' commandment to be judgmental toward others.

Second, when we are busy judging others, we can become prideful, gaining a false sense of holiness. I think each one of us can find plenty of things wrong with other people, especially people around us. But if we focus on finding the faults of others, we ignore the hard work of identifying our own faults and working on eliminating them. Unfortunately, some of the most judgmental persons are often very religious people who go through the motions of religious rituals on a regular basis. Tragically, their religious practices often make them blind to their own faults for they are too busy being religious and judging those who don't engage in their religious practices. Because they are often quite blind to their own judgmentalism, this evil is hard to eliminate.

And third, we should not judge others because we do not know where they are on their life journey. Like the four brothers who each saw the mango tree in a different season, we see people at particular points in their lives. I know some people who were absolutely delightful young people who grew up to be bitter people, just like I know some who had the opposite experience. People can change, and that is what our religion is all about. We are called to always be in the state of becoming holier and holier.

As we continue our life journey this week, it would be a good idea to take a hard look at our own lives. How do we judge others? Do we feel holier or superior to others?

And that is the good news I have for you on this Fifth Sunday of Lent.

Story Source: "Judgment in All Its Seasons." *Sower's Seeds That Nurture Family Values: Sixth Planting*, Ed. Brian Cavanaugh. 2000, #30, p. 39

Chapter 14

Palm Sunday of the Passion of the Lord - C
Holy Week

Scripture:

* Isaiah 50: 4-7
* Psalm 22: 8-9, 17-18a, 19-20, 23-24
* Philippians 2: 6-11
* Luke 22: 14 – 23: 56

Today, we begin the most special week of the year for Christians, Holy Week.

Today, we celebrate Palm Sunday of the Lord's Passion. We read not only the great welcome he received from the people, but we then learn how they turned against him when we hear the Passion according to St. Luke.

On Tuesday this week, the bishop and priests of the Diocese of Raleigh will gather at St. Andrew's Church in Apex to celebrate the annual Chrism Mass. At that Mass, the bishop and priests will renew their priestly promises, and they will bless the three oils that will go to each parish for the coming year. The oils will be used to celebrate various sacraments in the parishes.

At 7:00 p.m. on Holy Thursday, we will begin a special Mass called the Mass of the Lord's Supper. As the Mass begins, the Season of Lent officially ends, and we enter a three-day season called, Triduum. At this Mass, the people will bring the three oils blessed at the Chrism Mass to the priest, and the priest will wash the feet of some people just as Jesus washed the feet of his Apostles. The washing of the feet symbolizes the new form of leadership Jesus gave to his disciples, that is, to be the leader, one must be the servant of all.

On Good Friday, we commemorate Jesus' Passion and Death. At St. Mary's, we will have the traditional Catholic service that is in three parts: Reading of the Passion; Veneration of the Cross; and a Communion Service. The 2:00 p.m. service will be in English, and the 7:00 p.m. service will be in Spanish. The Hispanic community will have their annual "Via Crucis" or "Way of the Cross" at 4:00 p.m. on Good Friday.

On Holy Saturday, we will celebrate the one Mass that is permitted that day at 8:00 p.m. The Mass is in both English and Spanish, and at this celebration we will have the Blessing of the New Fire, Blessing of the New Water, Blessing of the Easter Candle, and most importantly, we will celebrate Sacraments of Initiation (Baptism, Confirmation, and First Communion) for many of the people in our RCIA Ministry.

On Easter Sunday, we will have our regular Sunday Masses plus a 6:30 a.m. Mass in English.

Try your hardest to attend as many of these special events as possible. You will be richly blessed.

And that is the good news I have for you on this Palm Sunday.

Chapter 15

Easter Sunday of the Resurrection of the Lord - C
Why Go to Church

Scripture:

- Acts of the Apostles 10: 34a, 37-43
- Psalm 118: 1-2, 16-17, 22-23
- 1 Corinthians 5: 6b-8
- John 20: 1-9

Today, Catholic Christians celebrate Easter, the greatest feast day of the Church Year. This feast is so great, in fact, that from the earliest days of the Church, Catholic Christians stopped celebrating the Sabbath (Saturday) as their day for the Lord, and switched it to Sunday, which they named, "The Lord's Day."

On behalf of the faculty, staff, and 6,000 anointed ministers of St. Mary Parish, I wish you and those you love a very Happy and Holy Easter!

Although Easter is about the Resurrection of Jesus from the dead, we should not look at Easter as simply an historical event to remember. On the contrary, this feast is about new life, about getting rid of the old self and rising to new heights. It is about growth and change. It is about shaking up our lives. For Catholic Christians, Easter is a truly Catholic story, for Catholic stories always have a "happily ever after" ending.

In our part of the world, Easter is a time when nature comes alive after the winter, and we see a profusion of new leaves on trees, flowers blooming and sunshine staying with us longer every day. It is as if the whole world is shouting "Alleluia!"

One of the ways that Catholic Christians are called to celebrate Easter is to examine our lives and clean our spiritual houses. For some of us, it means working on getting rid of bad habits or getting ourselves out of ruts we may be in. For others, it means adding exciting new practices into our daily lives. But today, I want to focus on something that many of us take for granted—coming to Sunday Mass.

The following story comes from many sources on the Internet, and it asks a very basic question: Why go to church?

> A church-goer wrote a letter to the editor of his local newspaper complaining that it didn't make sense to go to church every Sunday. He wrote,
> "I've gone for 30 years now, and in that time I have heard something like 3,000 sermons. But I can't remember a single one of them. Therefore, I think I'm wasting my time, and the pastors are all wasting their time by giving sermons at all."

This letter to the editor ignited a spirited controversy in the "Letters to the Editor" section of the newspaper. Naturally, the editor was delighted. The flood of letters, both pro and con about going to church on Sunday, went on for weeks. Then, however, one day someone wrote an incredibly wise letter that seemed to stop everyone dead in their tracks.

The wise writer wrote:

"I've been married for 30 years now. In that time my wife has cooked some 32,000 meals. But, for the life of me, I don't recall the entire menu for a single one of those meals. I do, however, know this. I know that each of the meals my wife prepared for me nourished me and gave me the strength I needed to do my work. If my wife had not given me these meals, I would be physically dead today. Likewise, if I had not gone to church to nourish my spirit, I would be spiritually dead today!"

So when you are down to nothing, God is up to something! Faith sees the invisible, believes the incredible, and receives the impossible! Thank God for our physical and spiritual nourishment!

This story is a good one for Easter, for it is designed for everyone here today. It is designed for those who come to church at least once a week and for those who come to church every day. It challenges those folks to stop taking this amazing gift for granted, to approach it in a more joyful way each day.

This is also a good story for those who come to church rarely. For them it is a challenge to give to the Lord one hour a week, an hour to slow down and say, "thank you" to the Lord for his many blessings and, "please" help me and my loved ones on their life journeys.

So, no matter who you are and what you bring to church this Easter Day, know that God loves you and will indeed nourish your spirits abundantly.

And that is the good news I have for you on this Easter Sunday.

Story Source: This story is found in many locations on the Web.

Chapter 16

2nd Sunday of Easter - C
Thomas' Palace

Scripture:

- Acts of the Apostles 5: 12-16
- Psalm 118: 2-4, 13-15, 22-24
- Revelation 1: 9-11a, 12-13, 17-19
- John 20:19-31

Today, Catholic Christians celebrate the Second Sunday of Easter, also known as Divine Mercy Sunday.

On this day, we read the interesting story of the apostle, Thomas. Because Thomas was not present when Jesus first appeared to the other apostles after he rose from the dead, Thomas had doubts. He didn't believe the other apostles when they told him that they had seen the risen Christ. But then, Jesus appeared again, this time with Thomas present. Thomas, upon seeing Jesus, said, "My Lord and my God!" From that experience, Thomas became known as "Doubting Thomas" throughout history.

There is a very interesting story about Thomas, however, that is much more positive. Though this is not an historical story, it is still a good one because it shows that the Church is made up of people, not bricks and mortar.

The story says that after Jesus showed himself to Thomas after his Resurrection, he sent Thomas to India to spread the good news of the gospel. Once he got to India, Thomas met a king who was interested in having a new palace built. Because the king liked Thomas, he gave Thomas money for materials and workers for the new palace.

Thomas, instead of hiring workers or buying supplies to build a new palace for the king, gave the money to the poor people he met. He also went through the kingdom telling everyone about Jesus and his life and death and resurrection. Many of the people Thomas met became Christians.

One day, the king asked Thomas, "Thomas, how is the building of my new palace coming along?"

"Oh, fine," replied Thomas. "It is being built up more and more each day." So the king gave Thomas more money, and Thomas promptly gave the money away to the poor whom he encountered.

This pattern went on for several weeks. The king would ask how the building project was coming along, and Thomas would tell the king that everything was fine. The king would give Thomas more money, and Thomas would promptly give it to the poor. Soon, pretty much everyone in the kingdom was Christian.

After a while, the king became very eager to see how the new palace was coming along, so he said, "Thomas, when can I see my new palace? Isn't it almost finished?"

Thomas kept putting the king off, assuring the king that it wasn't quite finished. Finally, however, the king said, "I want to see it today, this very minute!"

So, Thomas took the king on a long walk through the kingdom, pointing to various people and explaining how their lives had changed for the better. "What is this all about?" the king complained. "Where is my palace?"

Thomas explained, "Your majesty, your palace is all around you, and it is indeed beautiful. How sad that you cannot see it. I hope that in time you will be able to see it."

"What do you mean, you thief? What have you done with my money?!"

Thomas replied, "The new palace I have built with the money you gave me is made of the lives of your people. They are no longer poor, and now they believe in Jesus. They are the towers of your palace, for God lives in them. You, indeed, have a most magnificent new palace!"

The king was so furious with Thomas that he threw him in prison. The king was even thinking of putting Thomas to death. But then the king began to notice how the people of the kingdom had changed, how different they were now that they were Christians. His wife, the queen, began to tell the king about all of the things Thomas had taught her.

Through the queen, God touched the heart and mind of the king. Soon, the king released Thomas and became a Christian himself. Thomas had shown the king that Jesus was living in the lives of the people. The king also learned that it is better for a rich ruler to share his wealth with the poor and to live simply than it is for one to live in the fanciest palace on earth.

This story is very important for people of all ages, for it reminds us that "the church" is not about buildings and towers and other material things. Rather, "church" is about a people on a journey through this world to the next. For Christians, it is about loving God, loving our neighbors and loving ourselves. Only when we grasp that concept will we be able to see "the church" that exists all around us. If we fail to understand that "the church" is the people, then we will be as blind as the king was before he became a Christian.

As we continue our life journeys this week, how do we see "church?" How do we live out the triple-love commandment of Jesus Christ?

And that is the good news I have for you on this Second Sunday of Easter.

Story Source: Goodhue, Thomas W. "Second Sunday of Easter (C)." *Sharing the Good News with Children: Stories for the Common Lectionary*. pp. 245-246.

Chapter 17

3rd Sunday of Easter - C
Fr. Bill Woods, Maryknoll Martyr

Scripture:

- Acts of the Apostles 5: 27-32, 40b-41
- Psalm 30: 2 & 4, 5-6, 11 & 12a & 13b
- Revelation 5: 11-14
- John 21: 1-19

Today, Catholic Christians celebrate the Third Sunday of Easter. In the Gospel of John, we hear Jesus command his disciples to be missionaries and to be pastoral.

In commanding the disciples to be missionaries, he told Peter and his fellow fishermen to cast their nets into the sea. He said this after the men had fished all night and came up with nothing. They did as Jesus commanded, and they caught so many fish that they were not able to pull in their boats. The fish represents people, the sea represents the world, and the disciples represented missionaries. With God's help, the disciples were to go into the world and bring in human beings to the Lord.

In commanding the disciples to be pastoral, Christ told Peter, who represents all disciples, to take care of Christ's sheep. The sheep, of course, are you and me. Therefore, Christ was saying that the disciples were not only to recruit followers, they were to take care of them in a loving way once they were "in the fold," so to speak.

For over 2,000 years, Catholic Christians have tried to follow these commands. Being human, however, the Church has often made mistakes. But, instead of focusing on the mistakes it has made, today, I want to share the amazing story of one man whom God touched in a remarkable way. The man's name was Bill Woods.

Bill was born in Houston, Texas in 1931, and he was ordained as a Maryknoll Missionary priest in 1958. After his ordination, Fr. Bill was assigned to work in Santa Cruz Barillas, a town in western Guatemala near the sparsely populated jungle regions of Ixcán and Quiché.

Like many new Maryknoll missionaries, Fr. Bill came to his first assignment filled with all the hope, joy, and enthusiasm of a newly-ordained priest. Bishop John McCarthy, a close friend of Fr. Bill, said this of him: "Fr. Bill was a Texas cowboy for Jesus, ready to enjoy the open spaces of Guatemala, to ride horses, jeeps, airplanes, and motorcycles, and to teach the Indians about the Catholic faith."

While in Santa Cruz Barillas, Fr. Bill opened a woodcarving cooperative for about 25 poor Indian families and a clinic. But, Fr. Bill knew that he was only helping a small minority of the poor Mayan Indians. To make a more meaningful impact, he would have to help the Indians get their own land. Right at that time, the Guatemalan government began a program allowing poor peasants to settle in the inhospitable Ixcán, a jungle near Santa Cruz Barillas.

This new program inspired Fr. Bill to develop a colonization program in the Ixcán jungle, serviced by small airplanes, where the Indians would be flown into the jungle where they could carve out farms for themselves. Pilots could then fly their produce out of the jungles and sell it in local markets.

In 1965, Fr. Bill learned how to fly a plane and purchased 100 square miles of land between two rivers. He invited a lawyer to help with land titles and distributed equal-sized plots of land to the Indians. Fr. Bill made sure that the titles for the plots of land were registered in the name of the cooperatives he founded. That would make it impossible for the rich to buy out individual farms once the Indians had developed the land and made it profitable.

By 1975, 10 years after Fr. Bill learned to fly, he had three small planes to service the five cooperatives he had founded. He and his pilot friends had flown over 12,000 trips to and from the Ixcán. Approximately 2,000 families had been settled, forming five towns. Nurseries were set up, schools were built for the children, new plants were introduced, and over 1,000 head of cattle were being raised by the five cooperatives. Each of the cooperatives had a clinic with paramedics and nurses.

To meet the spiritual needs of the people, each cooperative had a chapel and meeting hall that were run by *Delegados de la Palabra* –"Delegates of the Word," – who run little Catholic churches in Central American nations in the absence of the priest. The Delegados provided religious instruction.

In the early 1970s, oil prices began to rise, and the Guatemalan government was ready to start drilling. Generals, favorable to the rich and the dictatorship of the government, set their sights on taking over the land developed by Fr. Bill and the Indians. When the army came to capture the land, many Indians fled in fright. Fr. Bill, however, did not back down. He took the case to the government and fought for the poor. As a voice for the poor and powerless, he was soon labeled as a troublemaker and marked for death.

Realizing that he was a target of the anti-Indian forces, Fr. Bill pointed to the sky over the jungle and said, "That is where they're going to get me one day."

On November 20, 1976, on a cloudless day, Fr. Bill took a physician, an American journalist, a lay missionary, and one other person to visit a cooperative in the Ixcán. Just after 11:00 in the morning, the plane crashed into a mountain. Suddenly, Guatemalan military, who "just happened" to be in this remote jungle area, quickly removed key engine parts that would have shown the plane had been shot down.

Fr. Bill Woods and lay missioner John Gauker were buried with honors in Huehuetenango. Thousands of Indians attended their funeral.

For over 2,000 years now, Catholic Christians have followed the missionary mandate of Jesus Christ. Martyrdom, rather than stopping missionaries, only emboldens them. That is why missionaries are often called "The Marines" of the Church.

As we continue our life journeys this week, it would be a good idea to reflect on those who are putting their lives on the frontlines of danger, spreading our Faith.

And that is the good news I have for you on this Third Sunday of Easter.

Story Source: Maryknoll Fathers & Brothers: "Father Bill Woods, Martyr of the Ixcán, Guatemala." 2013 Web.

Chapter 18

4th Sunday of Easter - C
St. Mary Sister Parish

Scripture:

- Acts of the Apostles 13: 14, 43-52
- Psalm 100: 1-2, 3, 5
- Revelation 7: 9, 14b-17
- John 10: 27-30

Today, Catholic Christians celebrate the Fourth Sunday of Easter. Often, it is also known as Good Shepherd Sunday because we hear Jesus referred to as a shepherd whose sheep hear his voice.

The Catholic Church throughout the world also uses this day as World Day of Prayer for Vocations. Although every Christian has a vocation, the Church focuses this day on vocations to the priesthood, the Religious Life, and to missionary activities throughout the world.

Usually when we talk about vocations or calling, we focus on the individual. However, collectively we are called the Body of Christ. Together, we are the eyes and ears and mouth of Jesus Christ. Together, we are called to do his work not only at home, but also in other places to meet the missionary mandate of Christ.

Our own St. Mary Parish has been known for over 100 years as a beacon of hope for the poor and a home for the immigrant. Founded primarily by Irish immigrants, today almost 20 percent of our parish is made up of immigrants from every continent of the world except Antarctica.

Today, I would like to report on how we, as a parish community, live out our missionary mandate via our sister parish ministry.

In 2008, we adopted a sister parish in the mountains of Honduras. This process is known as "parish twinning," and many missionary groups call this the "Third Wave" of missionary work in the United States.

The parish, called San Francisco de Asís, has 50,000 parishioners with 85 churches and chapels, and it is the largest parish in the Archdiocese of Tegucigalpa, the Capital of Honduras. Sixty percent of the communities of our sister parish do not yet have electricity, and the people are extremely poor. The parish has five main towns and more than 80 other communities. Many of the communities are so remote that the only way to get to them is via mule or horse. This parish is more like a diocese than a parish from an American perspective, and it has 1,000 Confirmations per year.

In addition to praying for each other, we take up a second collection for our sister parish twice a year. So, if you have given to this collection, or prayed for our sister parish, you are a part of this Sister Parish Ministry. This ministry is headed by Laura Vinson-Garvey who can accomplish more in a couple of days than a team can do in months.

There is a special group in the Sister Parish Ministry that devotes itself to raising funds for the health care projects of this parish. This group, called SaludHondu, is headed by Dr. John Cromer. Because our health care initiatives are expanding rapidly, this group's mission is vitally important.

We also established a medical clinic in the main town of Reitoca, and the people named it Clínica Santa María after our parish. Today, it serves 400 people a month and has a full-time physician, nurse, pharmacist, and jack-of-all-trades kind of person. The clinic staff plans to train health providers for the remote parts of the parish soon based on a model of Maryknoll Sisters, who are also American surgeons, in Guatemala.

While on a mission trip in April, the Mayor of La Libertad, one of the major towns of the parish, gave our sister parish a beautiful building to have a new clinic. The building is right on the town square. He also pledged to have a staff clean the building each day. Above the building is a house for a physician or other person to live.

We have also established an excellent relationship with a Rotary Club in Tegucigalpa called Kaputzihil. This Club is going to provide us with free medications for our clinics, and they want to pour money into the new clinic. They very much want to partner with the Wilmington Rotary Club.

With the money from second collections at St. Mary Church, the people have been able to rebuild churches that have washed away in floods, build restrooms, build a rectory for the two priests, put flooring in churches, paint churches, and do many other projects.

We also have regular immersion mission trips to expose parishioners to this exciting parish.

In the future, in addition to regular immersion mission trips, the St. Mary Sister Parish Ministry will sponsor mission trips for youth, construction workers, and health care professionals. I am looking forward to the Knights of Columbus to be involved in a special way as both priests of our Sister Parish will be Knights by this summer.

Currently, we are hoping that a Rotary matching grant can come through to buy a pickup truck for our Clínica Santa María. On our January mission trip, a woman died because there was no way to get her to the hospital, which is three hours away from Reitoca. When the priests came to the town from picking us up at the airport, they put a mattress in the back of their truck, laid her on it, and drove her to the hospital in

Tegucigalpa three hours away. Her 16-year-old son, with tears running down his face, stayed with her trying to soothe her as the truck made its way on the incredibly wild, unpaved mountain roads. She died at the hospital.

Because of our work in Honduras, and because parish twinning is considered the "Third Wave" of missionary work, I am extremely pleased to announce that the Maryknoll Mission Education Board has voted to make a film about St. Mary Parish, showing how an American parish not only does parish twinning, but how it does it right. I will keep you posted about its progress.

And that is the great news I have for you on this Fourth Sunday of Easter.

Chapter 19

5th Sunday of Easter - C
Fallen Away & Communion

Scripture:

- Acts of the Apostles 14: 21-27
- Psalm 145: 8-9, 10-11, 12-13ab
- Revelation 21: 1-5a
- John 13: 31-33a, 34-35

Today, Catholic Christians celebrate the Fifth Sunday of Easter. In the Gospel of John, we read about Jesus talking to his disciples, right before he left them for the final time. He commanded them to love one another. What Jesus was telling them, in effect, was that he lived in them. Therefore, how they treated each other was how they, indeed, were treating him.

This was the second time Jesus talked about himself being in another place. At the Last Supper, Jesus took bread and wine and turned them into his Body and Blood. He then commanded his disciples to take his Body and eat it, and to take his Blood and drink it. He then commanded that this action be carried out into the future.

For over 2,000 years, now, Catholic Christians have treasured this gift that Jesus gave us, the gift of himself. It is sometimes called the Blessed Sacrament, Holy Communion, or Eucharist. The word Eucharist, however, is also used to refer to the Mass itself.

Some people through the years, however, have lost sight of this beautiful gift, only to find out later how much they truly loved it. That is what happened to a young man named Craig.

One Sunday, when he was 18 years old, Craig announced to his family that he was not going to Mass with them that day. Craig's 12-year-old brother, Bill, was amazed. Craig's mother, a very staunch Catholic Christian angrily said, "You most certainly are going with us to Mass!"

But Craig's father, who was not Catholic, said, "No, he's 18 and old enough to make his own choices." Craig felt liberated now that he did not have to go to Mass on Sundays. Suddenly, Sundays were free for him.

It took Craig a while, though, to notice that he was not nearly as happy as he thought he would be. He felt off-balance. He felt something was missing in his life.

In his 20s, Craig began exploring various Protestant denominations— Episcopal, Evangelical, Methodist and others. He felt the rituals in them were somehow "lightweight" in nature. And, either they did not have Communion each week, or when they did, it clearly did not have the same meaning that he had been raised to understand as a Catholic Christian. He could not find a single Protestant church to satisfy the spiritual hunger he felt.

By the time he was in his 30s, Craig began exploring the Unitarian Universalist Church where one can believe in anything or in nothing. Soon, though, the group of Unitarian Universalists he had joined dwindled in number and then just dissolved.

In his 40s, Craig went nowhere on Sunday. He felt the term "fallen away" had new meaning, for having no place to find balance and guidance and a spiritual foundation was like falling.

Then, however, two important things happened in Craig's life.

First, his brother, Bill and sister-in-law began attending a new Catholic community. First, Bill got his parents to try out the new parish, and then Bill invited Craig to come. Craig liked the new community with lively music and an energized congregation. He like the priest, Fr. Fred, and was touched by some of things the priest said. Soon, Craig began to drift in and out of attendance at the Catholic parish.

The second thing that happened was that his father, who had defended his decision not to attend church many years earlier, decided to become a Catholic Christian. Craig, with his own family, was at the special Mass where his father was baptized and received his First Holy Communion from Fr. Fred.

That was the last little push Craig needed. He finally "came home" to his Catholic faith in his 50s. Now, he treasures the ritual of the Eucharist and treasures receiving Holy Communion. By the grace of God, Craig came full circle to his home.

This is a beautiful story and very relevant as we begin our First Holy Communion celebrations here at St. Mary Parish. I hope that each of you who are receiving Holy Communion for the first time will always treasure it. There is an old saying that if you always stay close to the Blessed Sacrament and receive it when you come to Eucharist, God will watch over you in a very special way all the days of your life.

Now, are there some who should not receive Communion when they come to Eucharist? Yes. The Church asks that those who have not received First Holy Communion should not receive it. The same goes for non-Catholics because Communion is a symbol of Christian unity, which we do not yet have. Also, those who believe they are in mortal sin should receive the Sacrament of Reconciliation first, and those whose marriages are not blessed by the Church should also refrain.

If you have some obstacle preventing you from receiving Communion when you come to the Eucharist, by all means contact me. Together, we can knock down those obstacles, though it may take some time.

And that is the good news I have for you on this Fifth Sunday of Easter.

Story Source: Strickland, Craig A. "Fallen Away." *Chicken Soup for the Soul: Living Catholic Faith*, Eds. Jack Canfield, Mark Victor Hansen, & LeAnn Thieman. Pneuma Books: Simon & Schuster, 2008. pp. 353-356.

Chapter 20

6th Sunday of Easter - C
Youth

Scripture:

- Acts of the Apostles 15: 1-2, 22-29
- Psalm 67: 2-3, 5, 6 & 8
- Revelation 21: 10-14, 22-23
- John 14: 23-29

Today, Catholic Christians celebrate the Sixth Sunday of Easter. In the Gospel reading of today, Jesus tells his disciples that he is leaving for heaven, and that his Father will send down The Advocate, the Holy Spirit, to be with them. Jesus, knowing that the disciples might be afraid of him leaving, says: "Do not let your hearts be troubled or afraid. You heard me tell you, 'I am going away and I will come back to you.' If you loved me, you would rejoice that I am going to the Father; for the Father is greater than I. And now I have told you this before it happens, so that when it happens you may believe'" (John 14: 27-29).

The Holy Spirit, about whom Jesus was talking, has been with the Church through the ages and is with each and every one of us now. We received the Holy Spirit in a special way at our baptism, and the Spirit has not abandoned us. Sometimes, however, we need to be reminded. We become afraid as we walk the journey of life on Earth.

Recently, I came across a beautiful essay by Samuel Ullman which reminds us, like Jesus does, to remain forever young, to continually look forward with joy and hope, not looking back with regrets and sorrow.

Youth

(Adapted)

By Samuel Ullman

Youth is not a time of life, it is a state of mind. It is not a matter of rosy cheeks, red lips and supple knees; it is a matter of the will, a quality of the imagination, a vigor of the emotions. It is the freshness of the deep springs of life.

Youth means a temperamental predominance of courage over timidity of the appetite, for adventure over the love of ease. This often exists in a person of 60 more than in a youth of 20. Nobody grows old merely by living a number of years. We grow old by deserting our ideals.

Years may wrinkle the skin, but to give up enthusiasm wrinkles the soul. Worry, fear, self-distrust bows the heart and turns the spirit to dust.

Whether 60 or 16, there is in every human being's heart the lure of wonder, the unfailing childlike appetite of what's next and the joy of the game of living. In the center of your heart and my heart there is a wireless station; so long as it receives messages of beauty, hope, cheer, courage and power from men and women and from the Infinite, so long are you young.

When the aerials are down and your spirit is covered with the snows of cynicism and the ice of pessimism, then you are grown old, even at 20, but as long as your aerials are up to catch waves of optimism, there is hope you may die young at 80.

Needless to say, this essay contains amazing wisdom. It reminds us to be young at heart, to focus on the now and future.

I am sure each of us knows people of the same chronological age who are vastly different in how they act and view life. I know priests who are old men at 45 years of age, and others who are young at 80. Those who act old frequently focus on the negatives of life. They talk about what a terrible place the world is and they long for the "good old days," the days of unbridled racism and polio and wars and other evils. Their young-hearted counterparts, however, rejoice at God's creation. They marvel at having the whole world at their fingertips via the Internet. They marvel at the swift pace of science and cures for disease. They are glad that the spotlight is finally being shone on the spiritual cancer of prejudice and discrimination, and they rejoice that the bells of freedom and equality in the world are beginning to peal. They are excited about the limitless possibilities of the human spirit.

It is truly amazing that any Christian, after listening to Jesus talk about the Holy Spirit being with us, could walk the highways and byways of life in fear. If we could just remember that God is with us every moment of every day, we would not worry so much about where we should live or where we should go to college or what occupation we should enter or whom we should marry. We would say, "I'm making the right decision with what I have at my disposal," make our decisions, and never look back with regret. If we fall down, so what. We simply say, in such cases, "What can I learn from this experience?" and then grow in wisdom and strength.

So what are your worries? What is the role of the Holy Spirit in your life?

And that is the good news I have for you on this Sixth Sunday of Easter.

Story Source: Ullman, Samuel. "Youth" (adapted). *Sower's Seeds That Nurture Family Values: Sixth Planting*, Ed. Brian Cavanaugh. NY: Paulist Press, 2000. #9, p. 15.

Chapter 21

Ascension - C
A Mother's Promise

Scripture:

- Acts of the Apostles 1: 1-11
- Psalm 47: 2-3, 6-7, 8-9
- Ephesians 1: 17-23
- Luke 24: 46-53

Today, Catholic Christians celebrate the Feast of the Ascension of Jesus into heaven after he had appeared several times to his disciples after his resurrection from the dead.

On this day, we read in the Gospel of Luke how, before he ascended into heaven, Jesus said, "And behold I am sending the promise of my Father upon you, but stay in the city until you are clothed with power from on high" (Luke 46: 49). The "promise" that Jesus was talking about was that God the Father would send down God the Holy Spirit upon the disciples. This event, which we will celebrate next week, would become known throughout history as the Christian Pentecost.

Because we are supposed to be God-like in our dispositions and actions, today we'll look at the concept of "promise" in our lives. To start, we'll look at a poem made by a new mother because in many nations of the Americas, including the United States, we celebrate Mother's Day in May. The poem is titled "A Mother's Promise" and was written by Nicole Seymour when she was eight months pregnant.

A Mother's Promise
By
Nicole Seymour

I promise to always love you in whoever you decide to be
I promise to be there for you, whenever you need me
I promise to not pass judgment without first hearing you out
I promise to be in your life from day one and to learn what
    you're about
I promise to keep you healthy and to help you grow nice
    and strong
I promise to teach you to be a good person and know what
    is right and wrong
I promise to protect you and to always know you are okay
I promise to always remember that being your mom is a
    gift, every single day
These words my angel are my promise to you
And during tough times I will read them through
To be reassured that what I am doing is right

And never giving up without a fight
You are now and will forever be,
My sweetest little boy. My baby.

This inspirational poem is a fine example of a special type of promise, the promise of one human to another. A promise is a commitment to do or not to do something. If you look into the field of promises, you will see there are many different ways of approaching the concept of promise. For simplicity sake, I will look at three basic types of promises: those made to God; those made to others; and those made to self.

The first type of promise is a commitment to God. At our baptism, for example, we commit ourselves to following Christ and his Church. Because most of us were too young to make this commitment for ourselves, our godparents did it for us. Another example of making a commitment to God is by vows or promises to live our lives in a particular way. People in Religious life, such as Brothers, Sisters, and certain categories of priests who are members of religious orders, make vows of poverty, chastity and obedience. Priests who are not members of religious orders make promises to live their lives in a particular way.

Second are promises we make to other people. These types of promises range from the extremely serious (such as making a promise of fidelity to another person at one's wedding ceremony or making a promise to our children to love them all the days of their lives no matter what), to the less serious type of promise (such as promising not to reveal that a particular person dyes her hair).

Unfortunately, many people make promises they repeatedly fail to keep. It is almost like the concept of promise is a hollow term. You and I all know such people. They are the ones who promise to show up to events and then bail out, usually at the last minute. They are the ones who say they will do something for you but fail to do so. They are the ones who are consistently late for everything. In short, these are the people in whom one cannot place his or her trust, for they are unfaithful.

The third type of promise is the commitment we make to ourselves. On New Year's Eve, for example, many people make such commitments. They promise to lose weight in the New Year and to exercise at the gym on a regular basis. Knowing this, gyms across America make a fortune in January. We know, however, that making a promise, and keeping a promise, are two different things. This is where the dictum, "The spirit is willing but the flesh is weak" comes into play.

As we continue our life journeys this week, it would be a good idea to reflect on the concept of "promise" in our own lives. What kind of promises do we make to God, others, and self? How faithful are we in keeping these promises?

And that is the good news I have for you on this Feast of the Ascension.

<u>Story Source:</u> "A Mother's Promise" by Nicole Seymour. www.FamilyFriendPoem.com.

Chapter 22

Pentecost - C
Great Heights

Scripture:

- Acts of the Apostles 2: 1-11
- Psalm 104: 1ab & 24ac, 29bc-30, 31 & 34
- 1 Corinthians 12: 3b-7, 12-13
- John 20: 19-23

Today, Catholic Christians celebrate the Feast of Pentecost, the birthday of the Catholic Church in particular and Christianity in general.

In the Acts of the Apostles, we hear, "When the time for Pentecost was fulfilled, they were all in one place together. And suddenly there came from the sky a noise like a strong driving wind, and it filled the entire house in which they were. Then there appeared to them tongues as of fire, which parted and came to rest on each of them. And they were all filled with the Holy Spirit and began to speak in different tongues, as the Spirit enabled them to proclaim" (Acts 2:1-4).

The Scripture continues to say that in Jerusalem at the time, there were many groups of people from various places who all spoke different languages. God made it possible for all of them to understand what the disciples were saying. Needless to say, they were all amazed at this miracle.

Now, of all the feasts of Christianity, none has the same flavor as Pentecost. Pentecost is all about excitement and energy and power and missionary fervor. It is about zeal and enthusiasm. It is like the launch of a rocket that nothing can stop.

Many Christians have tried to recapture this energy and fire of the Spirit. Unfortunately, however, they have mistaken the Pentecost experience for an emotional state of being. There are even some Christian denominations that attempt to recapture the Pentecost experience by working themselves into frenzied states with exuberant music, loud preaching, clapping, dancing and jumping around. While it is fun to treat ourselves to such energizing worship activities once in a while, we must remember that our religion is not based on emotion. Our religion is based on belief and hard, and often tedious, work. The work of the Spirit is often tedious and difficult. Being the eyes and ears and hands and mouth of Jesus is hard work. Meeting our missionary mandate is hard work. The great American poet, Henry Wadsworth Longfellow, captured this idea when he said, "The heights by great men reached and kept were not attained by sudden flight, but they, while their companions slept, were toiling upward in the night." Today, I give the example of one of the most challenging parts of ministry for many priests in the Diocese of Raleigh: Ministering in a language other than their own.

In the Diocese of Raleigh, all priests are expected to be able to celebrate Mass and the other sacraments in both English and Spanish. Although

Spanish-speaking immigrants are diligently studying English, praying to God is always the last thing to go when adopting a new language. For example, when I want to determine how acculturated children of our immigrant parishioners are, I ask them two questions, "When you talk to God in the privacy of your heart, what language do you use?" and, "When you are alone with your brother or sister at night in your room, what language do you speak?" Those two questions tell me everything.

Learning new languages are very easy for little children, for their brains are like sponges. For adults, however, learning a new language is hard work. The Holy Spirit does not come down and suddenly zap one with the ability to converse in a new language. Just ask any immigrant how difficult it is to learn a new language. Just ask any seminarian or priest how difficult it is to learn a new language. The average parishioner, when thinking of the work of the parish priest, usually doesn't think of the minutes, hours, days, weeks, months, years and, yes, even decades of painstaking work the priest puts into learning a new language so that he can serve the people better.

Now, in the seminary, one of my professors told us that "love covers a multitude of sins." In this context, he was talking about the idea that our future parishioners would forgive our mistakes in a language that was not our primary language. Far more important than speaking perfect Spanish would be our love for them. And, to a great extent, this is true. I know of many examples, some even right here in our diocese, where a Spanish-speaking priest has treated the Hispanic parishioners very poorly, while the English-speaking American priest loves them very much. The people know the difference.

But as everyone who is faced with ministering in a new language knows, love can only get you so far. If you need to know where the bathroom is, love is just not enough. You need to know the words for "where" and "bathroom."

Fortunately, although the Spirit does not pour a new language into our brains instantly, the Spirit does give us an absolutely critical tool in our quest for learning a new language – a sense of humor. Without humor, learning a language would be absolutely unbearable.

I remember, for example, when I was a seminarian studying Spanish in Guadalajara, Mexico. One day, I asked a young man I knew if he knew any

English. He replied, "No. The only English I know is what I absolutely need to know: I need you! I love you! I can't live without you!" We had a great laugh over that.

One also has to be able to laugh when one uses words incorrectly, such as going to a restaurant and ordering a "pescador" for dinner instead a "pescado," a "fisherman" instead of a "fish."

The moral of the story is that the work of the Spirit is work. Hard work. Work that demands not only great energy, but also perseverance over time. The work of the Spirit is not about "feeling good" all of the time. It is about facing challenges and failures, yet never giving up.

How is the Spirit working in your life? What kind of challenges do you have in your vocation? How does a sense of humor help you meet your obligations?

And that is the good news I have for you on this Pentecost.

Part 3

ORDINARY TIME

Chapter 23

Most Holy Trinity - C
Making Lemonade

Scripture:

- Proverbs 8: 22-31
- Psalm 8: 4-5, 6-7, 8-9
- Romans 5: 1-5
- John 16: 12-15

Today, Catholic Christians celebrate the Feast of the Most Holy Trinity. On this day, we are reminded that although we believe in only one God, we believe that in this God are Three Divine Persons—God the Father, God the Son, and God the Holy Spirit.

Although the concept of the Trinity is never mentioned in the Bible, there are many references to Three Persons. In today's reading from St. Paul to the Romans, for example, we read about Jesus (who is God the Son), "God" which in this context refers to God the Father, and the Holy Spirit.

In this passage, we receive a message that bears a second look. We read, "…we boast of our afflictions, knowing that affliction produces endurance, and endurance, proven character, and proven character, hope, and hope does not disappoint, because the love of God has been poured out into our hearts through the Holy Spirit that has been given to us" (Rom 5: 3-5). Today, in the United States, we have two sayings that capture this message. The first is, "What doesn't destroy you makes you stronger." The second is, "When life gives you lemons, make lemonade." In other words, the afflictions or struggles of our lives can help us to grow and flourish. That is exactly what we see in the life of Wilma Rudolph.

Wilma Rudolph was born the 20th of 22 children on June 23, 1940, into a poor African-American family that lived in the backwoods of Tennessee. She was born prematurely, and her survival was doubtful for a while. When she was 4 years old, she contracted pneumonia and scarlet fever that left her left leg paralyzed. Because of the paralysis, she had to wear an iron leg brace. Fortunately, Wilma's mother continually encouraged her by telling Wilma that she could do anything she wanted to do with her life. Her mother told Wilma that all she needed to succeed was faith and courage and persistence and a strong spirit.

As a child, Wilma would often take off her braces, and her brothers and sisters would take turns massaging her leg. Her mother, a domestic worker, drove Wilma 90 miles roundtrip to Nashville every week for therapy.

At the age of 9, Wilma finally got out of her leg braces for good. She began to walk and made remarkable progress that her physicians said would never happen. And when her brothers put up a basketball hoop in their yard when she was 11, Wilma became obsessed with playing basketball. She also got it into her head that she would become the greatest woman runner in the entire world.

At the age of 13, she entered a race and came in a very distant last place. She continued to enter every race she could in high school and, consistently, she came in last. All of her friends begged her to quit, but she refused. One day, however, she did not finish last in a race – she came in second-to-last. And from that day on, she became better and better. Soon, Wilma won every race she entered.

After graduating from high school, Wilma went to Tennessee State University. There, she met Coach Ed Temple. He saw that Wilma was no ordinary athlete. On the contrary, she had an amazing spirit and great natural talent. He worked with her so well, that Wilma went to the 1960 World Olympic Games in Rome.

In the 1960 World Olympics, Wilma won three gold medals in track and field, the first woman in history to win three such medals in a single Olympic Games.

Wilma Rudolph did not limit herself to winning at sports. Rather, she used her leadership abilities, passion and sense of justice to work for the civil rights for African-Americans. She also used her celebrity to encourage disadvantaged people to be successful in the world of sports.

On November 12, 1994, at the age of 54, Wilma Rudolph died of brain cancer in Nashville, Tennessee. NBC made a movie about her life called, "Wilma."

When we read stories about such amazing people, it is good to reflect on them because they indeed reflect the sacred Scripture. In looking at Wilma Rudolph's life in light of St. Paul's Letter to the Romans, we indeed see that affliction can lead to endurance, and endurance can lead to proven character, and proven character can lead to hope. Here are three things I think we can glean from the Scripture and the story of Wilma Rudolph.

First, the idea that dealing with afflictions can produce endurance and strength is well known. When athletes engage in strenuous physical exercise, they build muscle. Likewise, when people use a spiritual program to deal with an affliction, such as Alcoholics Anonymous to combat alcoholism, the result is often remarkable spiritual growth.

Second, when looking at Wilma's story, we see she had many people behind her, people such as her mother, her brothers and sisters, and her coach. Like Wilma, you and I have God behind us, rooting for us every step of the way. The Holy Spirit is alive and working in each of us to help us overcome all obstacles that may block our path.

And third, we need to remember that not every door we want to enter is meant for us to enter. Sometimes, God wants it closed to us because He has a different door in mind for us. Thus, we should never consider ourselves a "failure" when we try something and it doesn't work out.

As we continue our life journeys this week, it would be a good idea to reflect on how our struggles against adversity have made us stronger, more spiritual people.

And that is the good news I have for you on this Trinity Sunday.

Story Source: Anonymous. "Become What You Want to Be." *More Sower's Seeds: Second Planting*, Ed. Brian Cavanaugh. NY: Paulist Press, 1992. #40, pp. 42-43.

Chapter 24

The Most Holy Body & Blood of Christ - C
The Care Collector

Scripture:

- Genesis 14: 18-20
- Psalm 110: 1, 2, 3, 4
- 1 Corinthians 11: 23-26
- Luke 9: 11b-17

Today, Catholic Christians celebrate a 13th Century Feast called the Feast of the Most Holy Body and Blood of Christ. On this day, we celebrate the gift of Jesus' real presence in the consecrated elements of bread and wine that occur at every Eucharist or Mass. Sometimes, the Body and Blood of Christ is called Holy Communion, or the Blessed Sacrament, or even "the Eucharist." The word Eucharist, however, more accurately refers to the entire Mass, not just the consecrated elements.

Catholic Christians in our country often take the Eucharist and Communion for granted. We have plenty of churches, paved roads and good transportation. Basically, nobody in the United States lives so far away from a church where the Eucharist is celebrated on Sundays that they cannot make it. As a result of the good fortune that we have in the availability of the Eucharist, we sometimes begin to take it for granted. Some even receive Communion without really sharing themselves with the Lord. They forget that by sharing our problems with another, in this case Jesus, we make our problems much lighter. That is something that people in the following story by Leo Remington called, "The Care Collector" found out.

There was once a village that had a section where collectors of various things came to sell things. They discovered that if you collected enough of something, other people would begin to think that somehow what they collected was valuable. Then, they would buy some of what you had so that they, too, could be collectors. There were all kinds of collectors in the village. Some collected colorful glass bottles, others stamps or pots and pans. Others collected golf clubs or comic books or records or sports cards or fine china.

One fine day, an old man came into the village and headed to the collectors' section of town. He carried a backpack that didn't seem to be very heavy and established himself in a corner. Naturally, the other collectors were very intrigued by the newcomer, so they came to him and asked what kind of collection he had in his backpack. He replied that he only had his lunch and a raincoat in case it rained.

The collectors were amazed and said, "Then you are not a collector?"

He replied, "Oh, yes, I am definitely a collector. I collect people's cares."

When the people asked him to continue, he said, "I learned long ago that one of the things everyone has too many of, and constantly tries to get rid of, are cares, trials, burdens, sorrows, difficult times—things that weigh them down and make them sad. So, I offer to collect them by listening to them."

The other collectors doubted this could actually work, but the old man seemed harmless, so they left him alone.

Soon, many people began to visit the care collector. They would tell him their problems, and then he would ask if they felt better. Every time, they would say that they felt better by sharing their burdens with him. After each person unburdened their problems, he would pretend to lift a heavy burden from them and put it in his backpack.

One day, a very sad woman came into the village and said that she wanted to see the care collector. When she found him, she told him that she had come from a town where everyone was very sad because they had so many problems. Immediately, the care collector decided to go to the new village. Because nobody in the village wanted him to leave, he had to sneak out during the night.

Not long after the old man had left the village, a young man appeared in the village. When the people found out from which town he came – the very, very sad town – they all wanted to know if he had heard of the care collector who had gone there. The young man replied, "Of course I did! You must not have heard. The old man was wonderful for the people. He listened to their troubles, and soon everyone was happier. Their lives were changed for the better, for they had shared their problems. No longer did they have to travel through life burdened by such heavy weight.

"Unfortunately, that made the government officials jealous. They felt threatened by the popularity of the old man. So, they killed him."

The people were astonished to hear about the death of the care collector. Then the young man said, "I feel better telling you about this, painful though it was. It's like what the old man did. He listened and collected cares. That is exactly what I will do. I will go back to that town and be a care collector just as the old man was."

The people tried to talk the young man out it. They explained that the people of the other town might kill him, too. They explained that there were just too many cares and burdens in that town.

The young man said, "Exactly! Exactly! That is why I'm going. I will become a care collector."

In our life, Jesus is a care collector. He listens to us any time of day or night, and he never interrupts us. If we place our trust in him, no matter what weight we are carrying around, it doesn't seem quite so heavy. So the next time you receive Holy Communion when you come to celebrate Eucharist, be sure to share your problems with Him.

And that is the good news I have for you on this Feast of the Body & Blood of Christ.

Story Source: Remington, Leo. "The Care Collector." *More Sower's Seeds: Second Planting*, Ed. Brian Cavanaugh. NY: Paulist Press, 1992. #69, pp. 64-68.

Chapter 25

2nd Sunday in Ordinary Time - C
Clínica Santa María

Scripture:

- Isaiah 62: 1-5
- Psalm 96:1-2a, 2b-3, 7-8a, 9-10a & c
- 1 Corinthians 12: 4-11
- John 2: 1-11

Today, Catholic Christians celebrate the Second Sunday in Ordinary Time. On this day, we hear from St. Paul about the gifts that the Holy Spirit gives to each of us. Paul says, in his First Letter to the Corinthians, "There are different kinds of spiritual gifts but the same Spirit; there are different forms of service but the same Lord; there are different workings but the same God who produces all of them in everyone. To each individual the manifestation of the Spirit is given for some benefit" (1 Cor 12:4-7).

As Christians, we all know that God gives each of us different gifts, and all gifts we received are social in nature. That means that they are to be used for the common good. But life flies by so quickly for most of us that we rarely sit back and reflect on just how God is guiding us. We often imagine that life events are random and chaotic. But, when we stop and seriously reflect, we see God's hand guiding us in amazing ways. Today, I want to give a brief glimpse into how God has worked to create our new Clínica Santa María in the town of Reitoca, F.M., Honduras. This is the clinic of our sister parish of San Francisco de Asís.

Around the age of four, God planted the seed of ordained priesthood in me. From that time, there was never a doubt in my mind about becoming a priest one day. At the age of 13 God planted a missionary spirit in me, and at the age of 14 I left home with two companions to enter Maryknoll Junior Seminary in Pennsylvania to study to become a foreign missionary. We graduated in 1961 on the 50th anniversary of the founding of Maryknoll - the Catholic Foreign Mission Society of America. Little did I know, that 50 years later I would be the Pastor of St. Mary Church in the neighborhood where Maryknoll's Co-Founder, Servant of God Thomas Frederick Price, grew up.

My vocation journey is too complex to go into here, but sufficient to say, God was preparing me for a special kind of priesthood. In 1999, after being ordained for one year, the mission director of our diocese asked me to visit Central America to see the devastation that Hurricane Mitch had caused. While there, I met a Maryknoll priest, Fr. Dave, who was a pilot and friend of a fellow pilot, the Cardinal of Tegucigalpa.

I never forgot the poverty of the people in Central America, and I knew that one day I would somehow put the missionary spirit into action. Then one day in 2007, God sent a homeless man to the St. Mary community by the name of Marcelino. I got to know Marcelino, who lived in a homeless mission so that he could send all of his salary as a laborer to support his family in Honduras. When he heard that I was looking for a sister parish for St. Mary Parish, Marcelino said, "Padre, why don't you adopt my parish in Reitoca."

After visiting the parish of San Francisco de Asís in Reitoca, I established a formal sister parish relationship. I was intrigued with the vision of the pastor, Padre Carlos, who dreamed of one day having a clinic for the people. His successors, Padres Ivis and Gerardo, shared this vision.

In time, the Holy Spirit guided many people to turn this vision into a reality. Thanks to the amazing generosity of the people of St. Mary Parish, and the work of many people, the new clinic is up and running. Padre Gerardo named the clinic after our parish, Clínica Santa María, and the logo for it has the triple towers of our Basilica Shrine of St. Mary.

Today, this clinic is treating 400 patients a month, many of them in life-and-death situations. This is possible because many people have used, and are using, the gifts God gave them for the benefit of all. Laura and Val and many Honduran workers made windows and doors for the new clinic. Reitocan workers constructed a new roof. Pablo built a new house where the physician lives and where visitors from St. Mary Parish can stay. Marco, a young physician, works five days a week treating patients with Yesenia, the nurse. Suyapa is the pharmacist of the Clinic, and Arnulfo not only keeps the place spotless, he helps all through the day with whatever needs to be done. The four workers do not even take lunch breaks.

The Mayor of Reitoca sent trucks and men to Tegucigalpa to bring supplies that we had sent down by ship in containers, and the Cardinal of Tegucigalpa has given his blessing. Dr. John and Penny and many others are working here on the home front to raise funds, while Maryknoll Sisters, who are American surgeons, are providing the clinic with plans to train health providers for the remote mountain villages of this far-flung parish of 50,000 parishioners in 85 churches. Many people, some who choose to remain anonymous, give regularly to pay the salaries of the clinic staff. We formally blessed the clinic on January 9, 2013.

On the last day of my recent mission trip, we were going to the Marriott Hotel where we always spend our last night. We came up to a car that had a rosary symbol on the back window. I laughed and told how in the past, Clifton and I had seen a window on a mission trip with a rosary in one corner and Playboy bunny on another window. Just as I said that, the two other St. Mary Parishioners shouted, "Father, look!" Pulling up right beside us was a car with a large Playboy bunny symbol on its window. Someone said, "That must be Clifton letting us know he is with us on this trip."

Later, when we got to the Marriott, we met with a Rotary Club to see if they would partner with the Wilmington Rotary Club, of which I'm part, so that we could get a pickup truck for the physician of our clinic. Not only were they willing to do that, they informed us that since two of their members own pharmaceutical houses, our new clinic would have all the drugs it needs for free.

And that is the good news I have for you on this Second Sunday in Ordinary Time.

Chapter 26

3rd Sunday in Ordinary Time - C
St. Francis de Sales as Writer

Scripture:

- Nehemiah 8: 2-4a, 5-6, 8-10
- Psalm 19: 8, 9, 10, 15
- 1 Corinthians 12:12-30
- Luke 1:1-4; 4:14-21

Today, Catholic Christians celebrate the Third Sunday in Ordinary Time. On this day, we hear from St. Paul, as we do almost every week. In his first letter to the Corinthians, Paul reminds us that the Church is like a body. And like a body, every part must work together to work well. No part of the body should be seen as inferior or superior, for we need each part to function.

Paul's teaching is part of what we learned last week about everyone having different gifts from the same Spirit. Each gift is social in nature. That means that we are to use our gifts for the benefit of all - never hoard the gifts for ourselves alone.

When he thought of various roles each could play in building up the Kingdom of God here on earth, Paul thought of roles such as prophets, teachers, healers and administrators. Even today, we first think of religious sisters, priests, missionaries and such when we think of roles we can occupy to be part of the Body of Christ. However, every single one of us is called to be part of the Body of Christ, and we do this in a wide number of roles: mothers and fathers, students, single people and coupled persons, and workers in every conceivable occupation.

One role often overlooked that is very crucial in building up the Kingdom of God is that of the writer. After all, without Paul having done his writing, we could not even be talking about the ideas he put forward. It was Paul, the most influential writer in Church history, who laid the ideas for all of our Catholic Christian theology.

I first became aware of how powerful the role of writer was when I was in my early 20s. I was a senior in nursing school in Cleveland, and I had a most amazing instructor named Mrs. Welch. She was a Renaissance kind of person. In other words, she did not have tunnel-vision like some of the other instructors had. Though she was certainly knowledgeable about the art and science of nursing practice, she was also keenly interested in theater, literature, art, history, geography, politics, current events, and other aspects of the world around her. Because she was highly effective as a teacher, I quickly grasped that she was helping patients through the nurses whom she had taught. So while a nurse was caring for 30 patients, Mrs. Welch was, in effect, caring for hundreds of patients. It was then that I decided to one day become a university professor.

After earning a doctorate and post-doctoral degree, I entered academia in a Big Ten University - the University of Iowa. From day one, I learned that, although being a good instructor was nice, the main rewards did not come from teaching; the rewards came from research and writing. The thinking went like this: It is through research and writing that new knowledge is generated. Instructors take this knowledge and teach it to students who, in turn, become nurses and treat patients. Thus, while a nurse may treat 30 people at a time, and while instructors may treat thousands of patients through their students at one time, researcher-writers can treat hundreds of thousands of patients through their writing. Further, writing lives long after the individual dies, while the spoken word usually does not. Thus, the writer can influence many generations as St. Paul did. Once I grasped this concept, I began to write and, like a snowball going downhill, I have been unable to stop writing even though my writing is in a different field today.

I am astonished how many hours a week a parish priest must devote to writing. I am incredibly grateful to God that we have computers to help in this process.

One man who grasped the power of writing in the Church was St. Francis de Sales who lived from 1567 to 1622.

Francis became a priest in spite of his father's opposition. As a priest, he was responsible for trying to bring followers of Calvin back to the Catholic faith. After having many doors slammed in his face, Francis decided to make little leaflets explaining the Catholic faith in simple and warm terms. He would slide these under doors of houses whose doors had been closed to him. He converted tens of thousands of people through his writing. No wonder he is a patron saint of writers.

In addition to his writings, he was also a gifted preacher with a gentle spirit and great love of God. Through his writing and preaching, Francis, who eventually became the Bishop of Geneva, became noted for three things:

First, he taught the people that everyone could be a saint. Sainthood was not something reserved for desert hermits or others with highly unusual vocations. Rather, homemakers and common laborers could, and should, become saints. Nobody is predestined to failure.

Second, Francis de Sales' writing was simple in style. He wrote for the common person. Writing with simple words, rather than complex words, is the mark of a wise person. Often, new writers like to show off by using big words that hardly anybody understands. They quickly learn, however, that this is not a good idea.

And third, Francis believed very strongly in the idea that one can "catch more flies with a teaspoon of honey than with a barrelful of vinegar." If we want to draw others to Christ, to God and to the Church, we must do so with kindness, not with the raving and ranting of the fire-and-brimstone kind of preacher.

How often do we acknowledge the vocation of writer? Do we realize that behind every word we read, there was a writer?

And that is the good news I have for you on this Third Sunday in Ordinary Time.

Story Source: "St. Francis de Sales" in *Butler's Lives of the Saints: January*, Revised by Paul Burns. Collegeville, MN: Burns & Oates/The Liturgical Press, 1998, pp. 165-173.

Chapter 27

4th Sunday in Ordinary Time - C
A Mother Paraphrases Love

Scripture:

- Jeremiah 1:4-5, 17-19
- Psalm 71:1-2, 3-4a, 5-6ab, 15ab & 17
- 1 Corinthians 12: 31 – 13: 13
- Luke 4: 21-30

Today, Catholic Christians celebrate the Fourth Sunday in Ordinary Time. On this day, we hear the beautiful words of St. Paul in his First Letter to the Corinthians. Of all the parts of Sacred Scripture, this is the most popular one chosen by brides and grooms for their wedding ceremony.

In this passage, Paul talks about the superiority of love over all of the other virtues. In fact, Paul says that without love, all of our good works amount to nothing.

Unfortunately, however, the word "love" has so many meanings that it is often difficult to discuss it. For example, when I looked up the definition of love on the Internet, there were over 150 definitions! For simplicity sake, "love" in this homily refers to wishing the best for ourselves and others. In other words, it is seeing Christ in every person and then acting accordingly. Therefore, love should exist towards all people whether we "like" them or not.

As we read Paul's discourse on love, we discover that it is filled with an amazing number of things to consider. We could devote a lifetime to reflecting on just this passage. One woman who reflected on this passage and put it into practical, everyday terms was Mrs. Mervin Seashore. This is her paraphrase of St. Paul's discourse on love.

A Mother's Paraphrase of 1 Corinthians 13
By
Mrs. Melvin Seashore

Though I speak with the language of educators and psychiatrists and have not love, I am as blaring brass or a crashing cymbal.

And if I have the gift of planning my child's future and understanding of all the mysteries of the child's mind and have ample knowledge of teenagers, and though I have all faith in my children, so that I could remove their mountains of doubts and fears and have not love, I am nothing.

And though I bestow all my goods to feed and nourish them properly, and though I give my body to backbreaking housework and have not love, it profits me not.

Love is patient with the naughty child and is kind. Loves does not envy when a child wants to move to grandma's house because "she's nice."

Love is not anxious to impress a teenager with one's superior knowledge.

Love has good manners at home—does not act selfishly or with a martyr complex, is not easily provoked by normal childish actions.

Love does not remember the wrongs of yesterday and love thinks no evil—it gives the child the benefit of the doubt.

Love does not make light of sin in the child's life (or in her own, either), but rejoices when he or she comes to a knowledge of the truth.

Love does not fail. Whether there be comfortable surroundings, they shall fail; whether there be total communication between parents and children, it will cease; whether there be good education, it shall vanish.

When we were children, we spoke and acted and understood as children, but now that we have become parents, we must act maturely.

Now abides faith, hope, and love—these three are needed in the home. Faith in Jesus Christ, eternal hope for the future of the child, and God's love shed in our hearts, but the greatest of these is love.

This reflection by Mrs. Seashore is very clever. It makes us think of the ways we could reflect on the concept of love in our own lives. So as we continue our life journeys this week, it would be a good idea to reflect love in our lives. Do we wish the very best for other people? Are we jealous of others when they get more than we do? Do we put our love into action by our deeds? If someone opened our checkbook, would they be able to tell that we are generous people?

And that is the good news I have for you on this Fourth Sunday in Ordinary Time.

Story Source: Seashore, Mrs. Melvin. "A Mother's Paraphrase of 1 Corinthians 13". *Fresh Packet of Sower's Seeds: Third Planting*, Ed. In Brian Cavanaugh. NY: Paulist Press, 1994. #11, pp. 11-12.

Chapter 28

5th Sunday in Ordinary Time - C
Vocation Calls and Responses

Scripture:

- Isaiah 6: 1-2a, 3-8
- Psalm 138: 1-2a, 2b-3, 4-5, 7c-8
- 1 Corinthians 15: 1-11
- Luke 5: 1-11

Today, Catholic Christians celebrate the Fifth Sunday in Ordinary Time. On this day, we hear three short vocation stories. A vocation, in Catholic thought, refers to an inclination towards a particular state in life that Christians accept as a call from God.

When Christians talk about vocations, they are talking about two things. First, they are talking about the common call that all of us have as followers of Christ. Second, they are also talking about a particular way of life God is asking us to follow. The more I study vocations, the more I am convinced that it is usually wrong to talk about each person having "a" vocation. Rather, I think we have many vocations or calls such as whether or not we are supposed to be married or single and what kind of work we are supposed to do. Further, because we are living so much longer than in the past, we may have different calls at various times in our lives. I know many people who have been called to do amazing things with their lives after they have retired from their jobs.

In today's readings, we hear from Isaiah, Paul, and Peter. In each of their stories, they shared four common elements. First, they recognized the call from God. Second, they each believed they were very unworthy people. Third, they were each touched by God in such a way that they felt they were made worthy to serve. And fourth, they left what they were doing to follow the Lord with all their hearts.

But a vocation story is more than the call. It also involves a response. After all, God is calling everyone to many things, so that is not news. What is news, however, is how we each respond to the various calls God is making.

In this homily, we look at three ways that people have of answering God's call for them. Some of the people we will encounter here, we have already encountered in past homilies. When we hear these various types of calls and responses, we are forced to examine how we have heard and responded to God in our own lives.

First, there is the person who hears a specific call from God early in life and has no obstacles in their path to following this call. These persons follow that call without seeming to have any doubts about their vocation, ever. A person who fit this call and response pattern was St. Therese of Lisieux, sometimes called "The Little Flower." From the time she was a little girl, her father, who is up for sainthood himself right now along with his wife, would take Therese to see the convent of the Discalced

Carmelites. He would point to the convent and tell his daughter that very holy women lived there. Therese, according to her autobiography, never once had any doubts about her call to be a member of that community.

Therese entered the convent as a teenager and died at the age of 24. One of the things she gave the world was the idea of the "little way of spirituality" – doing even little things in life with perfection all for the honor and glory of God.

A second call/response pattern occurs in people who hear God calling them and answer enthusiastically, "Yes, Lord, here I am!" The Lord, however, has a winding and sometime torturous path for their vocation journey. God's answer to them is not, "No," but rather, "Not yet." This was my pattern to the priesthood. God had an amazing path for me to travel for what I imagine will be an exciting, unusual, and hopefully long priesthood.

One person we have encountered who followed this type of call/response was St. Rose Philippine Duchesne, a French Sister who came to the United States in the nineteenth century. When she was a little girl, Rose heard exciting tales of missionaries working with Native American Indians in the United States. That is what she wanted to do; however, God had different plans for her. When her convent was pretty much destroyed by the French Revolution, Sr. Rose's community joined another group of sisters who came to St. Louis, Mo when Rose was 49 years old. Rose's heart soared with hopes of finally being able to work with the Indians.

The bishop, however, said it was a mistake for the sisters to have made the journey. She and the other sisters endured many hardships of the frontier and did do much work with the poor, but not with the Indians. But, at the age of 72, Sr. Rose finally got to work with the Indians she had dreamed of for so many years. Unfortunately, though, she was unable to learn their language. In poor health, she decided to live among the Indians and devote herself to prayer for them. She became known as "Woman-Who-Prays-Always." Little Indian children liked to sneak up on her and sprinkle pieces of paper on her habit. When they came back hours later, the pieces of paper were undisturbed.

And then there is the call/response pattern in which God says, "No." That is what happened to St. Benedict Joseph Labré, an 18th Century French tramp. When he was a very young man, Benedict believed God was calling him to be a monk. However, after being rejected by many religious communities, he realized that was not his vocation. As a result, Benedict became a pilgrim, wandering around Europe visiting shrines and churches. As a homeless tramp, St. Benedict Joseph Labré showed the world that one can achieve great holiness in any way of life.

These are only three call/response patterns. There are more that I'll talk about another day.

For now, however, I ask you to reflect on your own calls from God. How did you know you were supposed to be in your line of work? For those of you who are married, did you ever ask yourself if this was God's will for you? If not, how did you know that was God's plan for you?

And that is the good news I have for you on this Fifth Sunday in Ordinary Time.

Story Sources:

"St. Therese of Lisieux." In *Butler's Lives of the Saints: October,* Revised by Peter Doyle. Collegeville, MN: Burns & Oates/The Liturgical Press, 1997, pp. 1-5.

"St. Philippine Duchesne." In *Butler's Lives of the Saints: November*, Revised by Sarah Fawcett Thomas. Collegeville, MN: Burns & Oates/The Liturgical Press, 1997, pp. 162-165.

"St. Joseph Benedict Labré." In *Butler's Lives of the Saints: April*, Revised by Peter Doyle. Collegeville, MN: Burns & Oates/The Liturgical Press, 1999, pp. 112-113.

Chapter 29

6th Sunday in Ordinary Time - C
Knock, Knock. Who's There?

Scripture:

- Jeremiah 17: 5-8
- Psalm 1: 1-2, 3, 4 & 6
- 1 Corinthians 15: 12, 16-20
- Luke 6: 17, 20-26

On this Sixth Sunday in Ordinary Time, we have some very interesting Scripture selections. In the passage from Jeremiah and from the psalmist, we learn that it is dangerous to place our trust in human beings. When we place our trust in them, we are like barren bushes in a harsh desert. But when we place our trust in the Lord, we flourish like a tree planted beside life-giving waters.

This theme is seen also in the Gospel passage that is sometimes called "the sermon on the plain." In this Gospel selection, Jesus reminds us that though we are enjoying good times in this life, it may not last. Likewise, though, when we are having very hard times in this life, they may not last either.

Taken all together, the Scripture teaches us to be humble, to place our trust in God and not get caught up in worldliness. That is what is emphasized in the following ritual in Austria. I call this story, "Knock, knock. Who's there?"

There is a church in Vienna, Austria in which the members of the former royal family of Austria are buried. When royal funerals arrive at the church for burial rites, the people leading the funeral procession knock at the door to gain entrance.

On the other side of the door is the priest. Through the locked door, the priest asks, "Who is it that desires admission here?"

The funeral procession leader calls out, "His apostolic majesty, the emperor!"

The priest replies, "I don't know him."

The funeral procession leader knocks a second time. Once again, the priest asks, "Who is there?"

Again, the funeral procession leader replies, "the highest emperor."

The priest again replies that he does not know such a person.

Finally, a third knock is made. This time, after the priest asks who is there, the funeral procession leader answers, "A poor sinner, your brother." Only with this answer does the priest open the door to welcome the people who want to conduct the royal burial ceremony.

This is a wonderful story that reminds us whatever we experience on this earth will not last. Those who are having a wonderful life will lose it just as surely those who are having a hard life. In the end, we all face eternity.

Most people, I think, can easily understand the Prophet Jeremiah and the psalmist when they talk about flourishing when we place our trust in the Lord instead of human beings. It is a little bit more difficult, though, to make sense out of Jesus' "sermon on the plain."

In the Gospel reading for today, Jesus says that the people who are "blessed" are those who are poor, hungry, hated, and weeping. On the other hand, he says woe to those who are rich and filled with food, who laugh and are praised by others. He promises that in the end the tables will be turned.

But are poverty and hunger and sadness intrinsically good? Is having people hate you good? Is being rich and filled with food truly bad? Is laughter intrinsically bad? Is having people like you bad? No. To understand this passage, we need the help of exegetes, experts in the Bible.

According to the exegetes, this passage was directed to followers and would-be followers of Jesus who led what we might call today "the good life." They had all that money could buy, and they were well-respected by society. What Jesus was doing in this sermon was not condemning them as a social class. Rather, he was challenging them. He was telling them not fall in love with the things of the world, things like money and power and prestige and good times. Rather, he was telling them to be thankful for what they had in this world, but to always be ready to share what they had with those who had less.

In this "sermon on the plain," Jesus was also telling those who had such a hard time in this world that in the Kingdom of Heaven, things would be different. In other words, he was teaching about hope and trust in the Lord rather than in the world. And what great news that must have been to those who had so little in this life.

The message for us Christians of today is clear. We are to be thankful for what we have. We are to remember that every good gift comes from God. This includes such things as our hard work and energy, our health and the people who taught us our values. This includes the country we live in and the opportunities that we have which the overwhelming majority of the people of this world will never enjoy.

We also must not get trapped by materialism, falling in love with the things of this life. We should own things, but never let things own us. And we should remember that every gift we have is to not only be developed and treasured, it is also to be shared with those in need.

When we can use our positions and gifts for the benefit of all our brothers and sisters, then we will have grasped the "sermon on the plain."

This week it would be a good idea to reflect on how we use our time, talent and treasure to help those in need.

And that is the good news I have for you on this Sixth Sunday in Ordinary Time.

Story Source: "Death of a Hapsburg" in William J. Bausch's *A world of stories for preachers and teachers*, #205, pp. 326-327, 1998.

Chapter 30

7th Sunday in Ordinary Time - C
Les Miserables

Scripture:

- 1 Samuel 26: 2, 7-9, 12-13, 22-23
- Psalm 103: 1-2, 3-4, 8 & 10, 12-13
- 1 Corinthians 15: 45-49
- Luke 6: 27-38

Today, as Catholic Christians celebrate the Seventh Sunday in Ordinary Time, we hear some extremely powerful directives of Jesus in the Gospel of Luke. Many people, Catholics and non-Catholics alike, do not want to hear what Jesus has to say because his message is so very difficult to follow. Therefore, many simply ignore Christ's commandments or pretend they do not exist.

Unfortunately, though, we are not called to "pick and choose" which commandments of Jesus Christ we are to follow, and which we are to disregard. So what exactly is Jesus commanding us to do in today's Gospel?

Jesus is commanding us to be kind to those who hate us. In fact, he goes so far as to tell us that if someone slaps us on one cheek, we should give the person our other cheek to slap. If someone wants our coat, we are to give them our shirt as well. If someone takes what is ours, something called stealing, we are not to demand it back. We are not to expect repayment when we lend someone money. We are to be compassionate and not judge others. We are to pardon others just as we want to be pardoned.

These are incredible commandments, commandments very difficult to follow. And because they are so difficult to follow, for more than two thousand years Catholic Christian thinkers have been trying to come up with reasons why we do not really have to follow them. They are what many call "Cafeteria Catholics," people who pick and choose what they will and will not follow.

The commandments of Jesus Christ are the commandments of Jesus Christ. They are written in black and white, whether we like them or not. And though they are incredibly difficult to follow, there is good news, for Jesus tells us that how we treat others is how God will treat us. If we truly forgive others and are compassionate, God will be sure to reward us. That is what we see in Victor Hugo's *Les Miserables.*

In that play, a man named Jean Valjean was released from prison where he had served for nineteen years. His crime was that he had stolen a loaf of bread to feed his sister's children. When he was released from prison, nobody would sell him food or give him shelter because of his prison record. Hopeless and exhausted, he stumbled into the house of a saintly bishop, who greeted him warmly and showed him remarkable hospitality.

Jean, continually suffering rebuke from others, could not understand the kindness of the bishop. Therefore, during the night, he stole the bishop's silver plates from the table. When the bishop awoke in the morning, he discovered that the dishes had been stolen by the stranger he had welcomed. But instead of feeling angry or sad about the loss, he was troubled by his own lack of charity. He reasoned that he should have sold the plates long ago and given the money to the poor.

As the bishop was thinking these things, the police arrived at his door along with Jean and the stolen plates. Before the police could talk, the bishop greeted Jean warmly and said, "My friend, I gave you the candlesticks along with the plates. Why did you not take them too?" The police, upon hearing that the bishop had given the silver pieces to Jean, reluctantly let the ex-prisoner go.

Jean Valjean stood in front of the bishop astonished. No one had ever treated him so kindly and compassionately. Then, to his further amazement, the bishop handed Jean the candlesticks and said, "Jean Valjean, my brother: You belong no longer to evil, but to good. It is your soul that I am buying for you. I withdraw it from dark thoughts and...I give it to good."

Although Jean Valjean meant his theft for evil, God and the bishop meant it for good. The rest of the book is about the good that can come out of transforming mercy.

Many of us, I am certain, are amazed at the words of Jesus and the story of *Les Miserables*. We can hardly believe that something so radical could possibly apply to us. But, either we believe that the words of Jesus apply to us as Christians, or we don't. It is that simple.

As the twentieth century came to a close and the twenty-first century began, there was a flurry of activity throughout the land among various right-wing groups. In their minds, the United States was losing its "moral compass" and becoming much too secular for them. Therefore, they came up with the idea of constructing monuments with the Hebrew commandments on them. Never, however, did they demand carving the Christian commandments on them. Never did they demand that we should love our enemies. After all, what would happen to war if we followed Jesus' commands? Never did they demand that we should give beggars whatever they asked for. After all, we would have to be abundantly generous with every "Tom, Dick, and Mary" who came along. They never demanded we not judge others. After all, what would happen to them and their self-righteous judging of those they consider morally inferior to them? Never did they demand we carve into stone the idea that we should not expect repayment when we give something to others. After all, what would happen to the money they make via interest payments?

This week, as we continue our life journeys, let's take some time to reflect on the words of today's Gospel. Do we truly believe they are meant for us? Why or why not?

And that is the good news I have for you on this Seventh Sunday of Ordinary Time.

Story Source: Anonymous, "Love your enemies," in Gerard Fuller's *Stories for All Seasons for Every Sunday, Every Year, Every Preacher, Every Teacher,* 1996, entry for 7th Sunday in Ordinary Time, Cycle C, pp. 114-115.

Chapter 31

8th Sunday in Ordinary Time - C
Kind Words

Scripture:

- Sirach 27, 4-7
- Psalm 92: 2-3, 13-14, 15-16
- 1 Corinthians 15: 54-58
- Luke 6: 39-45

As we come together today to celebrate the Eighth Sunday in Ordinary Time, we hear some very powerful words from the Book of Sirach about the nature of speech. In today's Scripture selection we read:

> The fruit of a tree shows the care it has had; so too does a man's speech disclose the bent of his mind. Praise no man before he speaks, for it is then that men are tested.

This is so very true. Have you ever met people who are strikingly handsome or beautiful - but when they open their mouths, and you listen to their conversation, they become so much less beautiful or handsome in your eyes? Likewise, have you ever met people who are not so strikingly handsome or beautiful who sparkle when you hear what comes out of their mouths? The more you get to know such people, the more attractive they become.

Our speech reflects the inner self. That is why it is so important. In the following essay by nineteenth-century English writer Arthur Helps, we get a glimpse into the nature of speech and its power.

Kind Words

Kind words are the bright flowers of earthly existence; use them, and especially around the fireside circle. They are jewels beyond price, and powerful to heal the wounded heart and make the weighed-down spirit glad.

Let us use our speech as we should wish we had done when one of us is silent in death. Let us give all the communications, make all the explanations, speak all the loving words ere it is too late.

A genuine word of kindness is often the best lever to raise a depressed spirit to its natural level.

The art of saying appropriate words in a kindly way is one that never goes out of fashion, never ceases to please, and is within the reach of the humblest.

Always say a kind word if you can, if only that it may come in, perhaps, with singular opportuneness, entering some mournful man's darkened room, like a beautiful firefly, whose happy circumvolutions he cannot but watch, forgetting his many problems.

What beautiful words this essay contains, words that show the power of speech. And it is good for us to hear such words from time to time, for often we forget just how powerful they truly are. Sometimes we misuse our speech, and, in the process, do no live up to our noble stature of children of God.

Here are three ways we can misuse speech.

First, we sometimes use vulgar or "dirty" words to express ourselves in everyday life. Now using such language is often a normal part of the rite of passage of children entering puberty. This has been especially important for male children to demonstrate their "masculinity." But today, as more and more females use such language, using such language is not such a mark of masculinity.

But there comes a time, however, when adolescents are supposed to grow up and become adults. The language we use as adults marks us. I remember one of my students at The University of Iowa saying in a class one day, "You know, people who never use bad language just glitter, they just glitter like diamonds." That has always stuck in my mind.

Second, we can sometimes misuse speech to kill or maim others' reputations. This is called gossip. In gossip, we steal others' good name and reputation without giving the ones we are talking about a chance to defend themselves. And like feathers in the wind, once the bag of feathers has been sown, they can never fully be recalled. That is one of the reasons gossip is such a deadly spiritual malady.

And third, we can harm others by unkind words. We can crush the spirits of children with our biting criticism and plunge adults into depression. On the other hand, kind words can lift spirits and provide wonderful elixirs for the soul. The old saying that we can catch more bees with a teaspoon of honey than with a barrelful of vinegar is so true.

As we continue our life journeys this week, it would be a good idea to examine our own speech. What comes out of our mouths, the mouths we use as entry points for Holy Communion?

And that is the good news I have for you on this Eighth Sunday in Ordinary Time.

Story Source: Arthur Helps, "Kind Words," in *Leaves of Gold,* edited by Clyde Francis Lytle, 1938, p. 158.

Chapter 32

9th Sunday in Ordinary Time - C
The Desert Pump

Scripture:

- 1 Kings 8: 41-43
- Psalm 117: 1, 2
- Galatians 1: 1-2, 6-10
- Luke 7: 1-10

As we gather to celebrate the Eucharist on this Ninth Sunday in Ordinary Time, we hear an amazing story of faith in the Gospel of Luke.

In this story, Jesus is entering Capernaum when some elders of a centurion came up to Jesus. They told him that a centurion who was very kind to the Hebrew people wanted Jesus to cure a servant of his that he held in high regard. Jesus, of course, was happy to grant the request. But as he got close to the house of the centurion, the centurion sent his friends to Jesus to tell him: "Sir, do not trouble yourself, for I am not worthy to have you enter my house. That is why I did not presume to come to you myself. Just give the order and my servant will be cured."

Jesus, of course, was astonished at the faith of this non-Jewish centurion, and he praised the faith of the centurion to the Israelites who were following him. Naturally, Jesus cured the man from a distance without even going into the centurion's house.

The first thing that probably strikes our ears as we listen to the words of the centurion is that the words sound familiar. And they should, for Catholic Christians say something very similar every time they come to Eucharist: "Lord I am not worthy to receive you, but only say the word, and my soul shall be healed."

But beside the humility shown in this selection, we also encounter the virtue of faith. Faith is easy to practice when we are on comfortable ground and everything is going smoothly, but when we are in times of trouble, it is not so easy to trust. That is the moral of the story told by Bruce Larson in his book, *Edge of Adventure*.

The story takes place in the Armagosa Desert, which is in Nevada near the Nevada-California border.

Once there was a weary traveler walking on a deserted trail in the Armagosa Desert. His water supply was gone when he came across a well pump. He frantically pumped the handle, but nothing happened. Suddenly, he saw a tin can tied to the pump with a note inside. The note said that the pump promises the only drinking water on this very long and seldom-used desert trail. The letter tells the reader that the pump was all right as of June of 1932. The letter writer goes on to say how he put a new leather sucker washer into it and how it should last for many years. But, the letter goes on to say, the leather washer has a tendency to dry out. Therefore, the pump has to be primed before using it.

Therefore, the letter continues, there is a bottle of water under a white rock close to the pump. There is enough water in the pump to prime the pump, but not if a person drinks it first. The directions tell the reader to pour about one-quarter of the water onto the pump and let it soak the leather for a bit. Then, pour the rest of the water medium fast and then pump rapidly. Then, the letter says, the traveler will get water. In fact, the letter continues, the well has never run dry, so the traveler should have faith. When the traveler drinks enough water, she or he should refill the water bottle and put it back under the white rock for the next traveler. The letter is signed, "Desert Pete."

Pete adds a postscript: "Don't go drinking the water first. Prime the pump with it first, and you'll get all the water you can possibly hold."

This is a very interesting story, isn't it? It provides us with a true dilemma. If we drink the water in the bottle from under the rock, we will surely have water. But if we follow Desert Pete's directions and use the bottled water to prime the pump, maybe it will work and maybe it won't. Should we cast our lot with a sure thing or should we cast our lot with faith?

Every day, Christians are faced with similar dilemmas. Most are not as dramatic as the traveler desperate for water on a deserted desert trail, but they are real nonetheless.

From the story of Jesus and the centurion, and the story of Desert Pete and his old well, we can glean a few things. Here are just three.

First, we should never be prideful about faith. Faith is a gift from God, but sometimes Christians forget this. They think they are responsible for having faith. As a result, they often look down on those without faith. But why would we look down on people just because they did not receive a gift? That makes no sense. Thus, we need to be humbly thankful for our faith and, as with all of God's gifts, we need to nurture and develop it.

Second, just because we have faith does not mean that everything will turn out the way we want it to turn out. For example, let's imagine that the weary desert traveler followed Desert Pete's directions. The traveler of course hopes that the well will still have water in it, but his wish does not make it true. Maybe the well does, and maybe it doesn't. His faith does not put water in the well. Therefore, we need to be ready for any consequences of our actions.

And third, sometimes we simply need to take a "leap of faith." People do this all the time. They examine a plan from all directions and come to the conclusion that they have to simply dive into an action plan. Taking a job in a distant place or entering a seminary would be good examples of leaps of faith.

As we continue our life journeys this week, it would be a good idea to examine our own faith life. What would we have done in the traveler's situation—drink the water from the bottle or follow Desert Pete's directions?

And that is the good news I have for you on this Ninth Sunday in Ordinary Time.

Story Source: "Desert Pete" in Wayne Rice's *More Hot Illustrations for Youth Talks*, 1995, p. 55.

Chapter 33

10th Sunday in Ordinary Time - C
Peak Experience

Scripture:

- 1 Kings 17:17-24
- Psalm 30: 2 & 4, 5-6,11 & 12a,13b
- Galatians 1:11-19
- Luke 7:11-17

Today, Catholic Christians celebrate the 10th Sunday in Ordinary Time. On this day, we read an interesting passage from St. Paul's Letter to the Galatians. In this letter, he tells his readers that before turning to Christ, he was a great persecutor of the Church. In fact, he was such a great enemy of the Church that he rose up the ranks in Judaism faster and further than many of his contemporaries. But, he then was touched by God, who gave him the insight to see he was to follow and preach Jesus to others.

As we know, no other writer of the Church has had a greater impact on it than St. Paul. Just about every single weekend, we hear a selection from St. Paul. His writings form the very foundation of our Catholic Christian theology.

Although there are many interesting aspects of Paul's Letter to the Galatians, today, we focus on how individuals can change on their life journeys. We see such a change in a story called, "Peak Experience."

Once there was a seeker who had a dream of one day climbing to the highest mountain peak. He believed that once he did that, he would be a success in his life.

To prepare for his long journey, he packed several boxes, a large backpack, and an overstuffed briefcase. Then, he began his ascent to the mountain peak. He was amazed at the beauty of the mountain and took joy in seeing various types of trees, flowers, animals and mountain streams.

But, as he climbed higher, he found he was becoming too tired carrying all of his belongings. Therefore, as he continued on his journey, he began to discard one box after another on the trail. Whenever he left a box behind, his burden became lighter, and he felt taller and more energized.

Finally, the man reached the peak of the mountain. He was amazed at his accomplishment, but he realized now that he had done this, it was time to go back down the trail and pick up the belongings he had left behind on the journey, and travel to a new valley, the valley of the future.

As he made his way back down the trail, he came across a large box, backpack, and an overstuffed suitcase. Picking up the first box, he noticed that it contained many memories, such as awards and report cards and even a piece of an old flannel blanket. He decided that he no longer needed these items to have memories, so he left the box on the side of the trail. Suddenly, he felt taller.

As he continued his way down the mountain, he came across the backpack he had earlier placed on the side of the road. In it, he found things of beauty that he had collected along his journey such as a piece of driftwood, a wooden sculpture, photographs of rainbows, and some favorite books. These, too, he left behind and continued his journey down the mountain.

He then came to the briefcase that he had left on the side of the road on his journey up the mountain. The briefcase was stuffed with various causes—issues and concerns that had inflamed his spirit and driven him to past actions. All of these seemed much less significant than they once were, so he left the briefcase by the side of the road and continued his journey down the mountainside.

Finally, he came to the last backpack on the side of the road. It contained a saw, a hammer, some other tools, and a bamboo flute. He slung it over his shoulder and continued his downward journey. Unfortunately, though, the backpack weighed him down too much and cramped his freedom. Therefore, he took out his flute and left the backpack behind. Now free of his belongings, he went his merry way, playing a happy song on his flute and entered the valley of the future.

This beautiful story is very relevant, for it ties into the human condition in a number of ways. Here are three things we can learn from this story and from the writings of St. Paul's life:

First, what we are like at one point in our life is not what we will be at another point in our life. St. Paul, formerly known as Saul, was an anti-Christian terrorist. Yet it was God who chose him to write the Scriptures that we Christians use as the foundation of our theology. Paul not only changed the direction of his life, he became a great saint.

Second, like the man who is ascending the mountain, many of us follow a similar pattern. We become collectors of things such as big houses, furniture, jewelry, cars and vacations and who-knows-what. We climb to the pinnacle of our profession and gaze at the world from the top. But, then we realize that that is all there is. It is no time to go back down the hill. Soon, we begin to de-clutter. We get rid of our big house and "downsize." We get rid of things we have stored in the attic, basement and garage, and strive to capture the simplicity we once had and treasured.

And, finally, we come to the golden years of our lives where sitting in a comfortable chair with a cup of coffee and newspaper becomes one of the most delicious moments of our day. We no longer need cruises and nightclubs and parties and noise to make us happy. We simply need a sense of serenity – peacefulness – to make us fulfilled.

As we continue our life journeys this week, what kinds of boxes and suitcases and backpacks and briefcases are we carrying through life that are weighing us down? Do we own these possessions? Or, do they own us?

And that is the good news I have for you on this 10th Sunday in Ordinary Time.

Story Source: Anonymous. "Peak Experience." *The Sower's Seeds*, Ed. Brian Cavanaugh. NY: Paulist Press, 1990. #36, pp. 1-33.

Chapter 34

11th Sunday in Ordinary Time - C
The Case of LaGuardia

Scripture:

- 2 Samuel 12:7-10, 13
- Psalm 32:1-2, 5, 7, 11
- Galatians 2:16, 19-21
- Luke 7:36 – 8:3

Today, Catholic Christians celebrate the 11th Sunday in Ordinary Time. On this day, we read an interesting passage in St. Paul's Letter to the Galatians about a concept called "justification." Paul says, "We who know that a person is not justified by works of the law but through faith in Jesus Christ, even we have believed in Christ Jesus that we may be justified by faith in Christ and not by works of the law, because by works of the law no one will be justified" (Galatians 2: 16). Paul goes on to say that "[...] if justification comes through the law, then Christ died for nothing" (Galatians 2: 21).

I think it is safe to say that most Catholic Christians do not speak about "justification." This concept, which has been a topic of great controversy among theologians for centuries, is simply not a hot topic for the average person.

Justification, in Catholic Christianity, refers to "God's gracious act of rendering a sinful human being holy and endowed with grace" (*The HarperCollins Encyclopedia of Catholicism*, 1995, p. 727). Before discussing the concept further, however, I begin with an interesting story of one of the most fascinating political figures in American history, Fiorello LaGuardia.

Mayor LaGuardia, when he was Mayor of New York City during the Great Depression and all of World War II, was nicknamed, "The Little Flower" by New Yorkers because he was only 5 foot 4 and always wore a carnation in the lapel of his sports jacket.

Brennan Manning, author of *The Ragamuffin Gospel* (Multnomah, 1990, pp. 91-92), notes that Mayor LaGuardia loved to ride in New York City fire trucks, raid illegal drinking establishments with the police department, take entire orphanages to baseball games, and even read the Sunday comic strips to children on the radio.

One bitterly cold winter night in January of 1935, Mayor LaGuardia went to the night court that served the poorest section of the city. After telling the judge to take the night off, Mayor LaGuardia took over the bench and became the judge for the evening.

Police brought a tattered old woman before him. She was charged with stealing a loaf of bread. She told the mayor that her daughter's husband had deserted her, her daughter was sick, and her two grandchildren were starving. The shopkeeper, from whom she had stolen the bread, refused to drop the charges. The shopkeeper said to the mayor, "It's a real bad neighborhood, your Honor. She's got to be punished to teach other people around here a lesson."

The mayor sighed. Then he said to the woman, "I've got to punish you. The law makes no exceptions—10 dollars or 10 days in jail." But as soon as he pronounced the sentence, the mayor reached into his pocket. He took out a 10 dollar bill and tossed it into the famous hat he always wore and said, "Here is the 10 dollar fine which I now remit. And, furthermore, I am going to fine everyone in this courtroom 50 cents for living in a town where a person has to steal bread so that her grandchildren can eat. Mr. Bailiff, collect the fines and give them to the defendant."

The next day, the New York City newspapers reported that $47.50 was collected from the people in the court and turned over to the poor and bewildered old woman. This money had been collected from everyone in the court that night including the store owner, policemen, 70 people charged with petty crimes, and people who had traffic violations. All of the people in the court gave the mayor a standing ovation.

This beautiful story reflects the nature of justification. Like the poor grandmother who stole bread to feed her children, she violated the law. The mayor, however, realized that her duty to feed her grandchildren was a greater duty than obeying the law. Thus, he fined her and then paid the fine.

In the concept of justification, Jesus died for our sins so that we would not have to. By his Precious Blood, we became "justified" or "made holy." By being made holy, we are now citizens of the Kingdom of God in a special way, not only here on earth, but also in Heaven.

Unfortunately, there have been many different schools of theology that have developed in Christianity that try to define the concept of justification. But, as we know, theologies come and theologies go. Theology, by its very nature, is the human attempt to explain and understand the Divine. Therefore, they are always suspect and subject to revision.

The important thing for Catholic Christians today is to realize that God loves us, and Jesus Christ gave his life for us. He was the Lamb who was sacrificed to wash away our sins.

And, as Catholic Christians, it is crucial to remember that we pray for the salvation of all human beings, not just selected ones. Our God is all-powerful, all-loving, all-merciful. We truly believe Jesus when he said, "With God, all things are possible." We believed Jesus when he said, "Ask and you shall receive." That is why Catholic Christians every day ask God, in his infinite power and mercy and love, to forgive the sins of all human beings—past, present, and future—and bring them to heaven for all eternity.

As we continue our life journeys this week, it would be a good idea to ask ourselves if we ask God for the salvation of all humanity each and every day.

And that is the good news I have for you on this 11th Sunday in Ordinary Time.

Story Source: Brennan, Manning. *The Ragamuffin Gospel*. Multnomah, 1990, pp. 91-92.

Chapter 35

12th Sunday in Ordinary Time - C
The Doughnut Story

Scripture:

- Zechariah 12:10-11; 13:1
- Psalm 63:2, 3-4, 5-6, 8-9
- Galatians 3:26-29
- Luke 9:18-24

Today, Catholic Christians celebrate the 12th Sunday in Ordinary Time. On this day, in his letter to the Galatians, St. Paul reminds his disciples that through our faith in Jesus Christ, we are children of God. He reminds the disciples that in baptism, they were clothed with Christ. Therefore, he says, "There is neither Jew nor Greek, there is neither slave nor free person, there is not male and female; for you are all one in Christ Jesus. And if you belong to Christ, then you are Abraham's descendant, heirs according to the promise" (Galatians 3: 28-29).

Unfortunately, it is very difficult for most of humanity to grasp the idea that all people are brothers and sisters because we have the same Creator. Likewise, it is difficult to grasp the idea that as followers of Christ, we are even more closely bound as special relatives.

Every once in a while, however, God sends us a sign to remind us to remember our common Christian fellowship. That is exactly what happened some years ago at a parish called St. Malachi in my hometown, Cleveland, Ohio. The parish is located on the lower West Side near what is known as, "The Flats" – an area near the Cuyahoga River that divides the East Side from the West Side, flowing into Lake Erie. At the time the story begins, The Flats was a very poor section of town. The river is probably most famous for catching on fire—three times—due to the pollution it once had from the steel mills.

One morning, many vagrants and other poor people were in line to get some coffee and doughnuts from the kitchen door at St. Malachi's rectory. Joining the line were two hungry little boys. One of them was very nervous, however, because he was not a Catholic. So when it was the boys' turn to ask for something from the priest, the non-Catholic boy said, "Maybe I can't have anything, Father, because I'm not Catholic." The priest smiled and said, "Well, young man, that is not a problem, because our doughnuts are not Catholic either." The priest, realizing the boys were too young for coffee, went into the kitchen and came back with milk to go with the doughnuts. Before leaving, the priest told the boys that whenever they were hungry, they would always be welcome at St. Malachi's.

More than a decade later, The Flats had become a very swank part of the city. People swarmed to the area to dine and party and live. One evening, my friend Sr. Donna Marie was on duty at the Rectory when the doorbell rang. When she answered it, there stood a young man with many trays filled with amazing delicacies such as shrimps, caviar, lobster tails, cheeses, meats, fruit, breads, and other things. He told Sister that when he was a little boy, he came to the rectory for food. He told how he had been very afraid because he wasn't a Catholic, but that the priest had told him that the doughnuts were not Catholic either. He told Sister how often he would come to St. Malachi's to get some food because his family was so poor and there was often no food for breakfast. He told Sister that he always intended to pay back the hospitality of St. Malachi's, and now he was finally able to do it as an employee of Windows on the River, a premier catering establishment on the banks of the Cuyahoga River.

The seeds of love that the priest had planted in the heart of the little boy fell on fertile soil. Now, the seeds showed through the young man's generosity toward the poor of the Lower West Side of Cleveland.

I love this story because it reminds me of something a nursing professor once told me. She said, "When you are just starting out in life, and someone helps you along the way, the way to pay them back is to help someone else on life's journey in the future." I never forgot that. Today, whenever I help someone on their life journey, I believe it's just part of "paying back" the generosity someone else showed me as a struggling young student. In other words, helping others is simply passing it on.

In Paul's discourse today, we hear that as Christians, we are challenged to show equality toward others. We are not to look at each other higher or lower, superior or inferior. Rather, we are called to see all as our brothers and sisters and then act accordingly.

The Church, through the centuries, has struggled with this commandment. Even today, there are people in high leadership positions that do not treat all people with dignity and respect. But, instead of focusing on the Church's many and shameful failures, I think it is better to focus on two more positive things: (1) its accomplishments in the area of love; and (2) the challenges we have in combating anti-love ideologies and behavior.

In the first area, we might focus on the progress the Church has made in combating racism and championing the rights of the poor. The social justice teaching of the Catholic Church is a model that many non-Catholic Christian groups use for their own denominations.

In the area of challenges, we can focus on the exciting changes the Spirit is calling us to fight for in many ways. By fighting for love over hate, and light over darkness, we will always have a purpose-driven life. Such a life in the Spirit is truly fulfilling.

As we continue our life journeys this week, it would be a good idea to reflect on how we see all humanity as brothers and sisters. What are we doing to create a Church and world free from prejudice and discrimination and other forms of hate?

That is the good news I have for you on this 12th Sunday in Ordinary Time.

Story Source: Sr. Donna Marie Bradesca, O.S.U. in a lecture, St. Mary Seminary, Wickliffe, Ohio, 1993.

Chapter 36

13th Sunday in Ordinary Time - C
If - By Kipling

Scripture:

- 1 Kings 19:16b, 19-21
- Psalm 16:1-2a & 5, 7-8, 9-10, 11
- Galatians 5:1, 13-18
- Luke 9, 51-62

Today, Catholic Christians celebrate the 13th Sunday in Ordinary Time. On this day, we hear an incredibly important message from Jesus about the quality of faithfulness to our vocations or callings.

In the Gospel from St. Luke, Jesus teaches us that once we set our sights on a goal, we must not be distracted from it. The primary goal that Jesus was referring to was to be a follower of him. To make his point, he told the man who wanted to go home to bury his father, "Let the dead bury the dead." And he told the one who wanted to first go back home to say farewell to his family before following Jesus, "No one who sets a hand to the plow and looks to what was left behind is fit for the kingdom of God." In both of these examples, Jesus was talking about being faithful to our Christian calling no matter what life throws at us.

One of the most famous American poems speaks to this message of fidelity or faithfulness to our calling. It is called "If" by Rudyard Kipling.

If

By Rudyard Kipling

If you can keep your head when all about you
Are losing theirs and blaming it on you;
If you can trust yourself when all men doubt you,
But make allowance for their doubting too:
If you can wait and not be tired by waiting,
Or, being lied about, don't deal in lies,
Or being hated don't give way to hating,
And yet don't look too good, nor talk too wise;

If you can dream---and not make dreams your master;
If you can think---and not make thoughts your aim,
If you can meet with Triumph and Disaster
And treat those two impostors just the same,
If you can bear to hear the truth you've spoken
Twisted by knaves to make a trap for fools,
Or watch the things you gave your life to, broken,
And stoop and build'em up with worn-out tools;

If you can make one heap of all your winnings
And risk it on one turn of pitch-and-toss,
And lose, and start again at your beginnings,
And never breathe a word about your loss:
If you can force your heart and nerve and sinew
To serve your turn long after they are gone,
And so hold on when there is nothing in you
Except the Will which says to them: "Hold on!"

If you can talk with crowds and keep your virtue,
Or walk with Kings---nor lose the common touch,
If neither foes nor loving friends can hurt you,
If all men count with you, but none too much:
If you can fill the unforgiving minute
With sixty seconds' worth of distance run,
Yours is the Earth and everything that's in it,
And---which is more---you'll be a Man, my son!

This beautiful poem speaks, I believe, to all of us. Every one of us has at least two vocations. Each of us is called to be a Christian, a follower of Jesus Christ. To be a follower of Jesus, we must base our behaviors on the triple-love command of Jesus, that is, to love God, love others, and love ourselves.

Each one of us, however, is called to specific ways of being a Christian. Some are called to be parents, for example, while others are called to a different path. Each adult is called to a specific occupation. But, whatever our callings, every one of us is challenged on our life journeys. Every one of us is tempted to give up from time to time. Every one of us is tempted to leave the path we are on to travel in a different direction. We sometimes call this temptation "the grass is always greener on the other side of the fence."

Each of us, I believe, wants to be faithful. We want to be good people. We want to be good workers and do our jobs well. Unfortunately, however, there are things that come up that can derail us if we are not careful. Almost always, the things that can derail us are other human beings. We go to work and it's filled with distractions. We fall in love but get burnt.

We do our best and have our intentions questioned. We invest our money and the stock market crashes. We move to a new city for a dream job and the company dissolves, leaving us in a strange town with no support system. We lose our loved ones. In other words, a million and one things can and do happen to us on our life journeys that can tempt us to give up, to look down instead of straight ahead. They tempt us to stop putting one foot in front of the other no matter what life throws at us.

Jesus, however, wants fidelity. He wants us to be faithful no matter what. So as we continue our life journeys this week, it would be a good idea to examine our own lives. What things challenge our fidelity our Christian and occupational vocations? How do we show we are faithful no matter what happens to us?

And that is the good news I have for you on this 13th Sunday in Ordinary Time.

Story Source: Kipling, Rudyard. "If." (This is found in many parts of the Web.)

Chapter 37

14th Sunday in Ordinary Time - C
Bl. Charles de Foucauld

Scripture:

- Isaiah 66:10-14c
- Psalm 66:1-3a, 4-5, 6-7a, 16 & 20
- Galatians 6:14-18
- Luke 10:1-12, 17-20

Today, Catholic Christians celebrate the 14th Sunday in Ordinary Time. On this day, Luke's Gospel, we hear Jesus' missionary commandment to the early disciples. He said, "The harvest is abundant but the laborers are few; so ask the master of the harvest to send out laborers for his harvest. Go on your way; behold, I am sending you like lambs among wolves" (Luke 10:2-3).

Jesus told this to his disciples while he was still walking among them. The good news of Jesus was not known throughout the world, so there was a great need for missionaries to go out and tell others about Jesus and his message of love for God, others, and self.

Through the centuries, the Catholic Church has striven to keep the missionary mandate alive both at home and abroad. But through the centuries, there have been other vocations that have developed in our Church. One of these vocations is a very fascinating, frequently misunderstood, and uncommon one: that of the hermit.

Just as a body needs a heart and brain to make the mouth and hands and arms and legs function, so, too, do missionaries need people praying for their work. That is one of the principle duties of hermits. Hermits are people who embrace the solitary life. In Catholic Christianity, the eremitic, or hermit, way of life has always been seen as an extremely sublime calling, one given to very few people.

Usually when we think of religious hermits, we think of people like St. Anthony of the Desert who lived long ago in Egypt. But the hermit vocation is alive and well even in our times. Today, I focus on a very interesting man who was not only a hermit, but a martyr.

Charles de Foucauld was born in Strasbourg, France in 1858. He was orphaned at the age of 6 when both of his parents died. His grandmother took him and his 3-year-old sister, Marie, in. However, tragedy struck a few months later. The grandmother and the two children were out walking when a herd of cows rushed toward them. The grandmother was so frightened, that she had a heart attack and died.

When he was in high school, Charles inherited much money and abandoned his faith. He joined the military and barely graduated from the military academy because he was lazy and led a wild lifestyle. He was not prone to obeying his military superiors and he kept a mistress.

While on a military mission in Africa, Charles fell in love with the desert and its solitude. In October of 1886, when he was 28 years old, Charles went through a conversion experience at the church of St. Augustin in Paris.

Four years later, in 1890, Charles became a Trappist monk in France and later in Syria. But in 1897, Charles decided he would rather serve the Lord as a hermit than a monk. In Nazareth, he lived near a convent of the Poor Clare nuns. When others suggested he should become a priest, he went to France where, in 1901 when he was 43 years old, he was ordained.

Following ordination, Charles returned to the Sahara Desert in Algeria and built a small hermitage near the Moroccan border and later, another hermitage in the central part of the Sahara Desert. For the rest of his life, he lived in Algeria close to the Tuareg people, sharing their life and struggles. In fact, he studied this people for 10 years, learned their language, made a dictionary and grammar book for them, and wrote about their language and cultural customs. In many ways, he was a modern-day anthropologist. In his hermit life, Charles de Foucauld called himself, "Charles of Jesus."

Charles' vocation, as he saw it, was to love. He wrote, "Let us concern ourselves with those who lack everything, those to whom no one gives a thought. Let us be the friends of those who have no friends, their brother. The love of God – the love of men – that is my whole life. That will be my whole life, I hope. When we can suffer and love, we can do much – the most that one can do in this world."

During his desert experience, Charles dreamed of founding a religious order. It was not until after his death, however, that the Little Brothers of Jesus was formed based on his writings.

On December 1, 1916, a group of armed bandits kidnapped Charles. When one of the bandits became startled by some intruders, he shot Charles through the head, killing him instantly.

Charles of Jesus was beatified by Pope Benedict XVI on November 13, 2005. The Algerian government honored his memory with a stamp, and many religious congregations have been founded as a result of his life and his writings. His feast day is December 1st, and he is honored as a martyr by the Catholic Church.

When we look at the life of Charles de Foucauld, we cannot help but be struck with amazement at how much of an influence a hermit could have on future generations of men and women who answered the Lord's call to serve Him in the priesthood or in the Religious Life. Charles de Foucauld's life also reminds all of us of the power of prayer and solitude for our spiritual journey.

As we continue our life journeys this week, it would be a good idea to reflect on our own lives. How do prayer and solitude enter into our life? How can we make more time for solitude to spend with Jesus?

And that is the good news I have for you on this 14th Sunday of Ordinary Time.

Story Source: "Charles de Foucauld." Wikipedia, January 2013.

Chapter 38

15th Sunday in Ordinary Time - C
Ryan's Wells

Scripture:

- Deuteronomy 30:10-14
- Psalm 69:14 & 17, 30-31, 33-34, 36ab & 37
- Colossians 1:15-20
- Luke 10:25-37

Today, Catholic Christians celebrate the 15th Sunday in Ordinary Time. On this day, we read one of the most famous and beloved stories in the Gospels – that of the Good Samaritan. In fact, it is so famous that even today we have Good Samaritan laws protecting people from lawsuits when they stop to help someone in distress.

In the story told by Jesus, we hear about a man who was robbed and left on the side of the road half-dead. Two pillars of the Jewish community, a priest and a Levite, passed by but did nothing to help the poor man. Then a Samaritan came along and cared for the man in a big way. The hero of the story was a Samaritan, a person whom the Jews despised. The listeners to Jesus' story learned two very important things. First, our "neighbor" is any human being in need. Second, the value of a good deed does not depend on who does it. Rather, it depends on the deed itself.

Today, we have many examples all around us of people who recognize a need and then seek to meet that need. That is exactly what happened to a 6-year-old boy named, Ryan Hreljac of Kemptville, Ontario, Canada. The story is told by Garth Sundem.

One day in 1998, Ryan learned in school about the children in Uganda, a very poor nation in Africa. He learned that the people there often did not have running water like they did in Canada. He learned that sometimes children had to walk more than three miles each way to gather water for their families, and even then, the water was usually unsafe to drink.

Ryan learned that many children had diseases from the water, and that one-fourth of the children had diarrhea at any one time. The teacher also told her first-grade class that $70 was enough to drill a new well in a town so that there would be enough water for an entire Ugandan village.

When Ryan got home from school, he asked his parents if they could give him $70. At first, his parents didn't take him seriously, but after a few days of Ryan's asking, they told him that they would give him extra chores to earn the money. Now, for a 6-year-old, $70 is a lot of money, but Ryan washed windows and picked up pinecones and did all kinds of chores. Although it took quite a while to earn the money, he finally did.

With great pride, Ryan went with his parents to an organization called WaterCan with the $75 he had earned. $70 was to drill a well, and $5 was so that the people who dug the well could have lunch. The WaterCan people were very pleased with Ryan's donation, but they explained that $70 would only buy a small hand-pump that sits on top of the well itself. They explained that it cost $2,000 to dig a well.

Instead of being totally discouraged, Ryan set out to raise $2,000 more. Now, this might seem like an impossible task for a 6-year-old. However, one day, Ryan's story was published in the local newspaper. Soon, people began sending checks made out to "Ryan's Well." The trickle of checks soon became a stream, and the stream soon became a river. Finally, a beautiful new well was dug in a village in northern Uganda.

This might have been the end of the story if Ryan had not been invited to attend a meeting of WaterCan one day. At that meeting, a man named Gizaw Shibru told the group that if he had a $25,000 drill, he could drill more wells in Africa. Ryan immediately said, "I will raise the money for that drill. I want everyone in Africa to have clean water."

Soon, the amazing story of Ryan Hreljac and his dream was published in newspapers all over North America. He was on television, including *The Oprah Winfrey Show*. The donations began pouring in and, eventually, millions of dollars were raised by the Ryan's Well Foundation. As a result of this foundation, new wells have been drilled in many nations of Africa, Asia and Central America.

In July 2000, Ryan got to see his work firsthand. As he drove into the town of Angolo in the back of his truck with his parents and Gizaw Shibru, Ryan was amazed when the children of the village shouted his name in greeting. The leader of the village told Ryan that thanks to him, the children were now healthy. All of this was due to the fact that Ryan recognized that all people in need were his neighbors.

This story reflects a very Catholic Christian view of reality.

First, it is Catholic in the sense that it has a universal perspective. It recognizes that neighbor is not bound by human-made borders. All people are our brothers and sisters, for we all have the same Creator.

Second, it provides a vivid example of how we are to be a "light to the world." We are to shine Christ through our actions much more than we are to shine Christ simply through talk.

And third, it shows how a small deed can grow into something much larger, just as an acorn can one day grow up to be an incredibly large oak tree.

As we continue our life journeys this week, it would be a good idea to take some time to reflect on how we serve our neighbors in need.

And that is the good news I have for you on this 15th Sunday in Ordinary Time.

Story Source: Sundem, Garth. "Ryan's Wells." *Real Kids, Real Stories, Real Change.* Minneapolis: Free Spirit Publishing, 2010. pp. 87-91.

Chapter 39

16th Sunday in Ordinary Time - C
Mary, Martha & Benedict

Scripture:

- Genesis 18:1-10a
- Psalm 15:2-3a, 3bc-4ab, 5
- Colossians 1:24-28
- Luke 10:38-42

Today, Catholic Christians celebrate the 16th Sunday in Ordinary Time. On this day, we hear the famous story of two sisters, Mary and Martha, who invited Jesus to dinner. When Jesus arrived, Mary sat chatting with Jesus while Martha was busy trying to get the dinner ready. Martha got angry at Mary because Mary was just sitting around while Martha did all the work. When Martha asked Jesus to tell Mary to help her, he replied, "Martha, Martha, you are anxious and worried about many things. There is need of only one thing. Mary has chosen the better part and it will not be taken from her" (Luke 10: 41-42).

Jesus' answer to Martha has caused much confusion through the centuries. Some people are definitely on the side of Martha, while others are on the side of Mary.

The pro-Martha side might say, "This is a story of hard-working woman named Martha and her lazy, deadbeat sister named Mary." The pro-Mary people might say, "This is a story of a calm, reflective woman named Mary and her neurotic, hyperactive sister named Martha."

There have even been people in the Church who have tried, with great arrogance and pride, to convince others that their lifestyle is superior to others. People in contemplative religious communities, for example, have falsely tried to take this story to convince others that their way of life is superior to those of missionaries and others who live a more apostolic life.

I believe, however, that this story has nothing to do with superior or inferior ways of life. Rather, I believe that it is designed to show that we need prayer and action in our spiritual lives. A life composed of just prayer would be inconceivable to a person in the monastic way of life, just as total action without prayer would be incomprehensible to parish priests and others who engage in apostolic work on a daily basis. The moral of the Mary-Martha story is that we need a strong prayer life as the foundation for our service work life. Service without a spiritual foundation is simply work, while service based on a firm relationship to God is ministry. There is a huge difference between the two. Mother Teresa of Calcutta showed that very idea one day. When an observer watched her doing some particularly disgusting work, the observer said, "I wouldn't do what you're doing for a million dollars." Mother Teresa said, "Neither would I!"

Unfortunately, human beings are prone to extremes. What is called for in a healthy spirituality is something known as balance. In the Religious Life, as well as in priestly formation, spiritual directors are forever talking about balance. They know that human beings have many life realms—physical health, mental health, leisure, family relationships, friendships, finances, work, school, spirituality, sexuality and others. Sound spirituality calls for maturely handling all realms of life. To do that calls for wisdom and prudence. It means that we don't permit any one life realm to get out of control, for if it does, we can suffer in all other realms, just as a human body can suffer when one body system goes bad. We don't have to look any further than asking a person who is in financial trouble just how pervasive this is in all of the other life realms.

One of the Church's most influential saints understood the importance of balance in a profound way. His name was Benedict, and he lived from 480-547 A.D. Though he came from a noble family, he never fell in love with things of the world. He was offended by the worldly behavior of his peers, and he sought to get out of Rome and its evils. He decided to live totally for God in peace.

As a young adult, Benedict gave up all of his father's wealth and privileged lifestyle and became a hermit. Although he prayed, he also worked to support himself. After three years living as a hermit, he was influenced by a friend to become the abbot of a local monastery. This, however, ended in failure when the monks of the monastery tried to poison him.

Once again, he tried to find peace in a cave, but God led him to leave the life of a hermit and take on the busy, social life of a monk. He founded several monasteries that held 12 monks each, and he wrote a rule for them to follow. This rule was based on prayer and work. Benedict knew that prayer without action was as ridiculous as work without prayer. For Benedict, work was not seen as a means to material gain. On the contrary, it was seen as something of beauty, a way of praising God. In the documents of the Second Vatican Council, this idea is restated when they talk of human beings being co-creators with God through our work.

The Feast Day of St. Benedict, called the Father of Western Monasticism, is July 11th.

As Catholic Christians, we are called to continually examine our lives. One of the greatest ways I have found to do this is through a life-realm approach. In this approach, we ask ourselves how we're doing in our friendships, in our finances, in our work, in our school, in our jobs, in our friendships, in our family and the like. When we want to focus more deeply on a life realm, we can delve deeper. For example, if we want to focus on our spiritual life, we can examine how we're doing in our prayer life, our stewardship, our spiritual reading, our virtue development, our vice reduction and the like. The process of growing and self-exploration is a fascinating and never-ending process.

As we continue our life journeys this week, it would be a good idea to reflect on our own lives. How do we balance prayer and service in our lives?

And that is the good news I have for you on this 16th Sunday in Ordinary Time.

Story Source: "St. Benedict." In *Butler's Lives of the Saints: July,* Revised by Peter Doyle. Collegeville, MN: Burns & Oates/The Liturgical Press, 1999, pp. 77-79.

Chapter 40

17th Sunday in Ordinary Time - C
President Lincoln Prays

Scripture:

- Genesis 18:20-32
- Psalm 138:1-2a, 2bcd-3, 6-7ab, 7c-8
- Colossians 2:12-14
- Luke 11:1-13

Today, Catholic Christians celebrate the 17ᵗʰ Sunday in Ordinary Time.

On this day, Jesus teaches his disciples how to pray by giving them the words that have come to be known as the Lord's Prayer or Our Father. But he goes beyond just teaching them a prayer. He tells them how important persistence in prayer is. This advice is for us just as much as it was for the disciples of his day.

In the following story, taken from George Bannister, we see the importance of persistence in action.

In the days when Abraham Lincoln was President of the United States, there was a great war between the states known as the Civil War. The North was loyal to the president, while the South was loyal to the Confederacy. The story takes place during the Civil War days.

There was a clergyman from New York who came to the White House to visit President Lincoln. When he got there he said, "I have not come to ask any favors of you, Mr. President. I have only come to say that the loyal people of the North are sustaining you and will continue to do so. We are giving you all that we have, the lives of our sons as well as our confidence and our prayers. You must know that no boy's father or mother ever kneels in prayer these days without asking God to give you strength and wisdom."

With tears in his eyes, President Lincoln replied, "But for those prayers, I should have faltered and perhaps failed long ago. Tell every father and mother you know to keep on praying, and I will keep on fighting, for I know God is on our side."

After chatting for a little while, the clergyman began to leave the room. President Lincoln held him by the hands and asked, "I suppose I may consider this as sort of a pastoral call?"

After the clergyman said, "Of course," President Lincoln said: "Out in our country, when a parson makes a pastoral call, it was always the custom for the folks to ask him to lead in prayer, and I should like to ask you to pray with me today. Pray that I may have the strength and the wisdom."

The two men knelt side by side, and the clergyman offered the most fervent plea to Almighty God that ever fell from his lips. As they arose, the president clasped the visitor's hand and remarked in a satisfied sort of way, "I feel better."

This is a beautiful story, for it ties in very well with Jesus' teaching on prayer. Sometimes, though, we take prayer for granted. We rattle off formal prayers, for example, without even thinking of what we're saying. This can happen especially when we engage in mantra-like repetition praying as in the rosary. Thus, it is good once in a while to stop and reflect on the nature of prayer. Here are just three points:

First, prayer is the act of human beings entering into a conscious, loving relationship with God. Sometimes our prayers are those of supplication or "asking" prayers. Parents often teach their children to pray for their parents and loved ones, including their pet dogs and cats. As children begin to grow, they begin asking God for help with studies in school or help with relationships. As adults, our asking prayers become more sophisticated, and we ask for intangible things for ourselves such as patience, wisdom or patience. We ask God for help in discerning our vocational paths in life, where we should live, and the grace to become better persons. We begin asking God to bless those we love in a special way.

As we grow older, we should find ourselves engaging in prayers of thanksgiving more and more. Unlike the child who sees God as Santa Clause, as adults we realize that all that we have is a gift from God, and God needs to be thanked for our blessings.

We also engage in prayers of adoration and asking for forgiveness of our faults.

Second, God answers all of our prayers. Having said this, we must remember that God does not always say "yes" to our asking prayers. Sometimes the answer is no. When I receive a no answer, I like to imagine that the actual answer is not no, but rather, "I am not letting you enter this door because I have a door that is infinitely more beautiful in mind for you."

Sometimes, God answers our prayers in a timeframe quite different from ours. Sometimes we want something immediately, but God wants us to undergo a long process before giving it to us. That is exactly what happened to me in my journey to priesthood. I was 100 percent certain that someday I would be a priest when I was 4 or 5 years of age. God, however, led me on an amazingly complex and winding journey before allowing me to be ordained at the age of 55. Looking back on my fascinating life, I realize that the long journey was actually a spectacular preparation for a very special priesthood, one that unfolds in mysterious and fruitful ways all the time.

And third, God wants us to continue to pray. He wants us to be persistent. This means that even when we don't feel like it, we are to pray. We are to pray even in the desert times of our lives, the times when our spirits are down, and we feel so alone.

As we continue our life journeys this week, it would be a good idea to reflect on our prayer life. How and when do we pray? How is our prayer life becoming richer in time?

And that is the good news I have for you on this 17th Sunday in Ordinary Time.

Story Source: Story is from a sermon by George Bannister, Praying for America, July 1, 2010 – found on Internet.

Chapter 41

18th Sunday in Ordinary Time - C
The Treasure

Scripture:

- Ecclesiastes 1:2; 2:21-23
- Psalm 90:3-4, 5-6, 12-13, 14 &17
- Colossians 3:1-5, 9-11
- Luke 12:13-21

Today, Catholic Christians celebrate the 18th Sunday in Ordinary Time. On this day, we have a rare treat when we encounter the three Scripture passages in that they all discuss the same concept: greed.

After hearing about the folly of becoming attached to things of this world in the Book of Ecclesiastes, and the "idolatry of greed" in Paul's letter to the Colossians, we hear what Jesus says about greed in the Gospel of Luke. In this Gospel selection, we hear about a man who had such an abundant harvest that he planned to tear down his barns so that he could build bigger ones. Then he thought he could sit back and "...rest, eat, drink, be merry!" But that very night, God took the life of this man. So what good did all the man's earthly riches do for him? It brought him nothing. Absolutely nothing.

Jesus then warns us that, "Thus it will be for all who store up treasure for themselves but are not rich in what matters to God" (Luke 12: 21). Needless to say, what matters to God is not the accumulation of material goods.

In the following story by a 19th Century Russian writer named Ivan Krylov, we hear about a man who was so greedy that it actually killed him.

Long ago and far away, there was a demon whose job it was to watch over a large treasure chest buried under an old house. One day, the demon was ordered by his superiors to leave for another part of the world. He would not be able to return to the old house for 20 years.

At first, the demon was worried because he did not want anyone to steal the treasure while he was gone for such a long time. But then he thought that perhaps he should hire a guard to watch over the treasure. But then he realized that hiring someone for 20 years would cost too much money. On the other hand, if he left it under the house, someone might come and dig it up. Finally, though, he came up with an idea that he knew would be foolproof.

He dug up the buried treasure and took it to the home of a man whom everyone knew to be a miser. "Dear Sir," the demon began, "I have been called to another country for my work. Because I have always been fond of you, I would like to give you a gift before I leave. I hope you don't refuse my offer. You should feel free to spend this treasure in any way you choose. The only stipulation I make is that when you die, I am to be your sole heir." The miser agreed, and the demon departed.

Twenty years later, after the demon had completed his assignment, he returned home to discover that the miser had died from starvation. The demon found the treasure, still intact in the strongbox. Not a single coin was missing. The demon laughed and laughed, knowing that the miser had chosen to die rather than spend a cent. The demon knew that the miser had been an excellent guardian of the treasure, and it hadn't cost the demon anything.

This is an interesting story for it shows how greed can be so powerful that it blinds people to what is important. And because Jesus spoke so many times to his disciples about the dangers of greed, it is always a good idea to reflect on this vice to ensure that it cannot take root in our own spirits. And if it has taken root, our reflection may help us make plans to free us from it.

Greed is an inordinate desire to possess wealth, goods or other things with the intention of keeping it for ourselves, far beyond the dictates of basic survival and comfort. Greed is often associated with an intense desire for power or status or wealth. In both the Old Testament books and New Testament books, we read how greed can destroy human beings and how it is related to other evils such as pride, disobedience and a lack of charity.

But if greed is evil, we might ask what its opposite is? The opposite of greed is generosity or moderation. Generosity means that we share what we have with others. Not only do we share such things as money, but we also share our experiences with others. We strive to help others advance through life. We do this when adults share their knowledge with younger people, trying to help them avoid the same mistakes they may have made on their life journeys. Peers show generosity when they provide others with helpful tips.

Though the concept of generosity is easily seen as the opposite of greed, it is not so easy to understand how moderation is an opposite of greed. Moderation, in this context, means that we use the things of this world wisely, but we do not fall in love with these things. In the Catholic Christian worldview, which is diametrically opposite of the fundamentalist worldview, the world and people are intrinsically good, for they were created by God. Therefore, we are to be thankful for material things, use them wisely, but not fall in love with them. We realize that we do not actually own anything in the material world, for one day we will die, and we cannot take any of it with us.

I have a priest friend in the Diocese of New Ulm in Minnesota who shows the concept of non-attachment in a beautiful way. Knowing that his family does not need money, he told me that he intends to leave any money he has to the parishes in which he has served, for that is where he earned the money. What a great concept that is!

As we continue our life journeys this week, it would be a great idea to reflect on our own spirits. Have we been afflicted with greed? How do we show generosity?

And that is the good news I have for you on this 18th Sunday in Ordinary Time.

Story Source: Krylov, Ivan. "The Treasure." *Stories for Telling: A Treasury for Christian Storytellers*, Ed. Brian Cavanaugh. NY: Paulist Press, 1986. pp. 113-114.

Chapter 42

19th Sunday in Ordinary Time - C
300 Gold Coins

Scripture:

- Wisdom 18:6-9
- Psalm 33:1 & 12, 18-19, 20 & 22
- Hebrews 11:1-2, 8-19
- Luke 12:32-48

Today, Catholic Christians celebrate the 19th Sunday in Ordinary Time. In today's Gospel reading from St. Luke, Jesus continues to teach his disciples about the importance of not becoming attached to this world, but rather, to continually remember that heaven is our true home. Jesus said, "Do not be afraid any longer, little flock, for your Father is pleased to give you the kingdom. Sell your belongings and give alms. Provide money bags for yourselves that do not wear out, an inexhaustible treasure in heaven that no thief can reach nor moth destroy. For where your treasure is, there also will your heart be" (Luke 12:32-34).

Although most of us, I believe, understand this message, the glitter of this world sometimes blinds us to the truly important things. We forget that we are just passing through this world on our way to heaven. That is what happened to the man in the following story by a French writer named Jean De La Fontaine.

There was once a cobbler who was a very happy, contented man. People loved to pass by his little shop because they loved to hear the cobbler singing at the top of his voice while he fixed shoes. Often, people just stopped in his shop to be warmed by the cobbler's radiant smile and laugh.

Now in this same town, there was another man who was a banker. Unlike the cobbler, he rarely smiled and rarely sang. He also did not sleep well at night. The banker did, however, observe the happy cobbler. At first, he was irritated by the constant good humor of the cobbler. However, as the days passed, he became attracted to the cobbler. He wondered what made the cobbler so happy all the time. So, one day, he decided to visit the cobbler to see if he could learn the cobbler's secret to happiness.

After the two men had talked for a while, the banker asked, "Are you wealthy? Pardon me for asking, but how much money do you make each year?"

The cobbler replied, "I'm not at all wealthy, but my family is seldom in want. Some days, I only fix shoes and do not sell any. I close the shop on holy days, so there is no income when we celebrate the feast of a saint. I simply cannot give you an exact amount that I make, but it is enough for me to feed and clothe my family."

"How wonderfully simple that is!" said the banker. "Because you have shared the secret of your success with me, I want to give you a gift. I am going to eliminate your financial problems for the immediate future. Take this gift of 300 gold coins and use them whenever you have need."

The cobbler was overjoyed. After the banker had left the little shop, the cobbler ran home and buried the coins in a corner of his house. But the days that followed brought many changes in the cobbler's life. The cobbler often found himself leaving the shop to go home in the middle of the day when his family was away, for he was afraid that someone might come and steal the coins. He began to lose sleep at night because he feared that maybe people were plotting to steal the treasure. Old friends noticed that he did not sing with the same cheer, and he seemed suspicious when someone stopped by the shop just to visit.

Finally, the cobbler visited the banker with the bag of gold coins in his hands. The cobbler said, "Thank you very much for the generous gift, but I cannot really afford to be the owner of these gold coins. Please take your money back so that I may again enjoy music, sleep and my friends. It seems that when I buried the money, I buried happiness at the same time."

From that moment on, the cobbler went back to his old self, and the town and the world were a better place because of it.

This is a wonderful story to have today, because it ties in closely with the Gospel message of Jesus. Here are three principles that we can glean from these messages:

First, Jesus cautions us to "not worry." As you know, this is easier said than done. We've all heard people say, "Worrying won't solve a thing" or "Worry won't make the problem go away." Worry, in itself, is anxiety. This can be both useful and harmful.

Worry is useful when it spurs us into action. If we are worried about what will happen to our children if we die, for example, we should be spurred into buying some term life insurance to protect them. If we're worried about an upcoming driver's license exam, then that should help us get the manual and study. These are examples of the positive effects of worry.

What Jesus was talking about, however, was lacking in God's providence for us. In other words, he was cautioning us that God is in charge and he loves us. When we truly grasp this, we should not worry so much.

Second, Jesus challenges us to examine our lives and determine where our true treasure lies.

And finally, we are challenged to use the things of this world wisely, but never fall in love with them. That is what Jesus meant when he challenged us, in many ways, not to be greedy or stingy with our money and other worldly possessions. Rather, we are to remember we are only passing through this world, and nothing of the material world can we take with us to the next.

As we continue our life journeys this week, it would be a good idea to ask ourselves where our treasures lie.

And that is the good news I have for you on this Nineteenth Sunday in Ordinary Time.

Story Source: Three Hundred Gold Coins" by Jean De La Fountaine. In William R. White's *Stories for Telling: A Treasury for Christian Storytellers*, 1986, pp. 112-113.

Chapter 43

20th Sunday in Ordinary Time - C
The Poison Cake

Scripture:

- Jeremiah 38:4-6, 8-10
- Psalm 40: 2, 3, 4, 18
- Hebrews 12:1-4
- Luke 12:49-53

Today, Catholic Christians celebrate the 20th Sunday in Ordinary Time. In today's Gospel reading from St. Luke, Jesus gives his disciples some very disturbing news. He tells them he has not come to bring peace the world, but rather division. The message of division is one that we often ignore. We continue to name churches "Prince of Peace" and talk about peace on earth at Christmastime. But all we have to do is look around to see that peace, which in religious context means harmony, is often absent. In Christianity, for example, we see incredible fractures. Not only are there divisions between Catholic and Orthodox Christianity, there are over 25,000 denominations in Protestant Christianity. Religious scholars believe there are five new Protestant denominations forming every week in the world. And when we look at Catholic Christianity, we see incredible strife based on a wide variety of issues.

In families, just as Jesus predicted, there is religious conflict. Parents are often devastated when their children choose a different religious path, and marriages sometimes dissolve because of religious differences.

In the following story called, "The Poison Cake," we see how strife can hurt others even when we don't mean to hurt them.

Long ago and far away, there was an old woman who lived in a forest by herself. Though she preferred to be by herself, she did see people sometimes. Whenever that happened, she spoke in proverbs that either baffled or irritated them.

One time, for example, when she saw people dressed in their finest clothes, she said, "A good name is to be preferred to great riches." And another time, when she saw a group of children getting into trouble, she said to their parents, "Train a child in the way he should go, and when he is old he will not depart from it."

Sometimes, the old woman would visit the home of a rich Polish prince landlord when she came into the village. If she saw him sitting in the sun she would say, "As a door turns on its hinges, so a sluggard turns on his bed." Or she might say, "For lack of wood the fire goes out." Although the prince always gave her food, he hated her.

One day, when the old woman came into the village, she encountered the prince in a very heated argument with another man. She stepped in between the prince and the person he was arguing with, shook her finger at the prince, and said, "A hot-tempered man stirs up strife, but he who is slow to anger quiets contention." From that moment on, the prince vowed to get rid of the old woman once and for all.

The next time the old woman visited the prince, he baked a cake full of poison for her. After talking pleasantly with her for a while, he said, "I have this delicious cake for you. You have probably never tasted such a wonderful cake before."

Instead of thanking the prince for his gift, she said, "One day you will find yourself."

As the old woman walked away from the prince's house, the prince muttered to himself, "And today, you will find yourself right in the arms of the angel of death."

On the same day the prince gave the old woman the poison cake, the prince's young son was participating in a hunt near the old woman's house in the forest. Unfortunately, the prince's son and his servants lost their way in the forest. Soon, they found themselves at the old woman's hut. After they knocked on the door of the old woman's hut, she welcomed them inside. After telling her how hungry and thirsty they were, she offered the prince's son a piece of cake and something to drink. The prince's son hungrily took a piece of cake and died after the first bite. The servants immediately left to bring the prince to his dead son. As the prince knelt at the side of his son, with tears streaming down his face, the old woman said, "the man who makes holes falls into them himself."

The moral of this particular story is that when we seek to harm others, we get harmed ourselves. Some have called this karma or, "what goes around comes around."

None of us should be surprised at the lack of peace in Christianity, for that is what Jesus predicted. Peace, for Christians, refers to harmony. We lack harmony not only in our beliefs and styles of worship, we lack harmony in our basic values. Instead of all following the triple love command of Jesus, many in Christianity have proclaimed hate to be a Christian value. Some Christians do this blatantly as is the case of the notorious anti-gay Westboro Baptist Church of Topeka, Kansas, while others do this in a much more hidden, but just as deadly, way.

But rather than focusing on the effects of Christian conflict, it would be good to take some time to focus on ways in which we can begin to get along. Some of the ways Christians have successfully overcome conflict is through ecumenical services on days such as Thanksgiving. Others get together to help the poor as we do in our St. Mary ministries that are open to all. And some do it in working on projects benefiting the whole community.

As we continue our life journeys this week, it would be a good idea to ask ourselves how a lack of peace on our Christian journey has affected us. How are we trying to establish peace in our hearts, homes, and parish?

And that is the good news I have for you on this 20th Sunday in Ordinary Time.

Story Source: "The Poison Cake." *Stories for Telling: A Treasury for Christian Storytellers*, Ed. William R. White. Minneapolis: Augsburg Press, 1986. pp. 123-124.

Chapter 44

21st Sunday in Ordinary Time - C
Matthew's Discipline

Scripture:

- Isaiah 66: 18-21
- Psalm 117: 1, 2
- Hebrews 12: 5-7, 11-13
- Luke 13: 22-30

Today, Catholic Christians celebrate the 21st Sunday in Ordinary Time. In today's New Testament reading from St. Paul's letter to the Hebrews, we encounter a theme that we rarely discuss in church—discipline.

After quoting a passage on discipline from the Old Testament, St. Paul says, "Endure your trials as 'discipline;' God treats you as sons. For what 'son' is there whom his father does not discipline? At the time, all discipline seems a cause not for joy but for pain, yet later it brings the peaceful fruit of righteousness to those who are trained by it" (Hebrews 12: 7, 11).

Discipline has many meanings. In this context, discipline refers to shepherding others to follow a particular path. If the sheep wander from the path, the shepherd takes certain measures to bring the sheep back to path. The purpose of all of this is harmony or peace.

Sometimes, sheep continue to wander, and the shepherd needs to take different or firmer action. That is what we see in a story by Walter Wangerin, Jr. It is about how he had to discipline his son in a variety of ways before his son stayed on the correct path.

There was once a father named Walter who had a son named Matthew. One day, Walter walked into his son's room. There, he found Matthew sitting on his bed with a big stack of comic books. Walter asked, "Where did you get all these comic books?" Matthew said, "I took them from the library." "Did you check them out of the library, or did you simply take them?" asked Walter. The boy said, "I just took them." "That means you stole them" said Walter.

So, Walter called the library and told the librarian that he was going to march his son Matthew right down there to return the books and to apologize for stealing them. Walter took his son to the library where Matthew returned the books and apologized for stealing them. The librarian gave little Matthew a stern lecture about stealing.

The following summer, Walter took his family on vacation to a small town in the State of Vermont. In the town, there was a little general store. After their summer vacation was over, the family returned home. One day, Walter walked into his son's room to find Matthew with a big collection of comic books. When asked where he had gotten them, Matthew told his father that he had stolen them from the store in Vermont during the summer.

Walter took little Matthew into the den and started a fire in the fireplace. He then threw in the comic books, one at a time, into the fire. With each comic book, Walter reminded little Matthew about the Seventh Commandment, "Thou shalt not steal."

A year later, Matthew once again stole some comic books. This time, though, instead of simply talking to Matthew, Walter said, "This time, son, I will have to spank you." So, Walter took Matthew into his study, took him over his knee, and spanked him five times with his bare hand. He felt that five times was just right. Walter figured that if he spanked him less than five times, it would be too little. If he spanked him more, he might get carried away and do too many.

After the spanking, Walter sat little Matthew down on the chair. Matthew hung his head. Walter knew that Matthew was trying hard not to cry, and he knew that Matthew did not want to shed a tear in front of his father. So, Walter said, "Matthew, I'm going to leave you alone for a while, but I'll be back in a few minutes."

After he stepped out of the room, Walter began to cry for his son. It broke his heart to see little Matthew sitting there so dejected. It broke his heart that he had to hurt his son like this. After he had cried pretty hard, Walter washed his face and went back into the den to talk with to his little son Matthew.

Years later, when Matthew was a teenager, he and his mother were driving back from a shopping trip, and they were reminiscing about the past. Matthew reflected on how he used to steal comic books. He said to his mother, "You know, after that incident with Dad, I really never stole anything again." His mother said, "I suppose the reason was because your father spanked you."

"Oh, no," replied Matthew, "it was because when he stepped out of the room, I could hear him crying."

This is a beautiful story because it reflects what Paul was saying today. All of us have heard at one time or another a parent say, "This is going to hurt me more than it hurts you." As children, we definitely do not believe it. It is only when people grow up and become parents themselves that they realize how true this is.

What we need to learn today is that the purpose of discipline for the Christian is to help keep us on the correct path. When we walk on the path of the Lord, we walk in harmony with God's plan for us. And harmony, as we have seen in the last few weeks, means "peace." Thus, peace occurs because we are in harmony with God.

As we continue our life journeys this week, it would be a good idea to reflect on our own lives. How does God discipline us? How do we grow from these difficult lessons and become better people?

And that is the good news I have for you on this 21st Sunday in Ordinary Time.

Story Source: Wangerin, Walter Jr. "Matthew." *A World of Stories for Preachers and Teachers*, Ed. William J. Bausch. 1998, #38, pp. 132-133.

Chapter 45

22nd Sunday in Ordinary Time - C
Humility & Booker T

Scripture:

- Sirach 3: 17-18, 20, 28-29
- Psalm 68: 4-5ac, 6-7ab, 10-11
- Hebrews 12: 18-19, 22-24a
- Luke 14: 1, 7-14

Today, Catholic Christians celebrate the 22nd Sunday in Ordinary Time. On this day, we get a very clear message from God to be humble people. In the Old Testament reading from the Book of Sirach, for example, we are told: "My child, conduct your affairs with humility and you will be loved more than a giver of gifts. Humble yourself the more, the greater you are" (Sirach 3: 17-18a).

In today's Gospel selection, we find Jesus at the home of one of the leading Pharisees. He couldn't help noticing how so many of them were choosing places of honor at the table. This led him to tell a parable about how it is so much better to take a lower place at the table. That way, you would not be in the embarrassing position of being asked to take a lesser place should a more important guest arrive. He sums up his teaching about humility when he said, "For everyone who exalts himself will be humbled, but the one who humbles himself will be exalted" (Luke 14: 11).

Often, it is easier to talk about humility when we see it in action, so here is a story of a man who exhibited this virtue in a beautiful way.

The story takes place in the 1880s in the State of Alabama. In those days, Booker T. Washington, a noted African American educator, was named president of the Tuskegee Institute there.

One day, as the new President of the Institute was out for a walk in an exclusive part of town, a wealthy white woman stopped him. Not knowing his identity, she asked him if he would like to earn a few dollars by chopping wood for her. Because he had nothing pressing at the moment, he smiled and agreed. He then began working. After he had chopped a good amount of firewood, he faithfully carried the logs into the house of the woman and stacked them up by the fireplace. A little girl recognized him, and later she told the wealthy woman who the man was who had chopped her wood.

The following morning, the wealthy woman, extremely embarrassed, went to see Mr. Washington at his office. When she got there, she apologized profusely to him. Booker T. Washington smiled and replied, "It is perfectly all right, Madam. Occasionally I enjoy a little manual labor. Besides, it's always a delight to do something for a friend."

The woman was amazed at Mr. Washington's response and told him that his meek and gracious attitude had endeared him and his work to her. Not long afterward, the wealthy woman showed her admiration by persuading some of her wealthy friends and acquaintances to join her in giving thousands of dollars to the Tuskegee Institute. The institute that Booker T. Washington led continues to thrive today as Tuskegee University.

Humility is a virtue, and a virtue is a good habit that allows us to perform actions with ease. Like any behavior, the more we practice it, the better we become at it. Just as emergency room nurses learn to perform cardiac pulmonary resuscitation without even thinking, we should strive to practice virtues automatically.

Humility is the virtue by which we know our place and take it. St. Thomas Aquinas, a great expert on virtues, said that humble people are balanced. In other words, they are not prideful about their talents, but on the other hand, they do not put themselves down either. They know what they're good at and what they are not good at.

One way to explore a virtue is to examine its opposite. The opposite of a virtue is a vice. There are three common vices that are enemies of humility: arrogance, false humility and judgmentalism.

First, arrogance is seen when people continually boast about their accomplishments. Instead of realizing that all their accomplishments could only have been achieved by the gifts that God gave them, they brag about themselves. They delude themselves into thinking that the source of their accomplishments is themselves and not all of the gifts that God gave them such as their parents, cultural capital, brains, desire for hard work, abilities and the like.

Second, some people have the vice called "false humility." Some have this vice because they truly believe they are intrinsically evil. They forget that they are children of God, and that God loves them and always will. At one point in Catholic Christian history, this vice was actually encouraged, and people engaged in very negative things such as self-mutilation and staying away from Holy Communion because they saw themselves as too unworthy. Others use false humility as a way of fishing for compliments. We see this in a straight-A student who says, "I'm sure I'll flunk the test," knowing that others will counter this with, "Oh, no, I'm sure you'll do well. You're the smartest student in the class." This type of false humility is a form of pride, the deadliest of all vices.

The third enemy of humility is judgmentalism. Judgmental persons see themselves as morally superior to others. They see themselves as holier and wiser. Frequently, they engage in exaggerated pious practices in church, causing attention to be diverted from the Body of Christ to themselves. Such people are often very arrogant, angry and hostile persons.

As we continue our life journeys this week, it would be a good idea to reflect on our own lives. How do we practice humility in our lives? Who do we know who is a good example of a humble person?

And that is the good news I have for you on this 22nd Sunday in Ordinary Time.

Story Source: Story of Booker T. Washington from Internet.

Chapter 46

23rd Sunday in Ordinary Time - C
A.A. & Detachment

Scripture:

- Wisdom 9: 13-18b
- Psalm 90: 3-4, 5-6, 12-13, 14 & 17
- Philemon 9-10, 12-17
- Luke 14: 25-33

Today, Catholic Christians celebrate the 23rd Sunday in Ordinary Time. On this day, we encounter an extremely challenging passage from the Gospel of Luke. In this passage, Jesus tells his disciples that anyone who does not hate his family and his very self cannot be his disciple. He also tells them that anyone who does not renounce all of his possessions cannot be his disciple.

Fortunately, Catholic Christians are not biblical literalists. We don't for a minute believe that Jesus wants us to hate our children, our spouses, our parents. On the contrary, we are to love all people, for the triple love command of Jesus himself is the very foundation of our Faith. We believe strongly in loving God, neighbor and self.

Likewise, we do not believe we must give away all of our possessions to be a true follower of Jesus.

If we do not take the command of Jesus to hate and renounce all of our possessions literally, how can we make sense of this part of the Gospel of Luke? We make sense of this passage, as we do for the entire Bible by asking ourselves, "What is the moral of the story? What was the theme or concept Jesus was trying to teach? How are we then to apply this theme in our lives so that we can be true followers of Jesus?"

The principle theme Jesus was trying to teach his followers was that of "detachment." Detachment is a theme common to every religion with which I am familiar. In the spiritual life, detachment refers to preventing or liberating ourselves from a harmful relationship to a person or a thing. In this definition, note that it is not the person or thing that is harmful. Rather, it is our relationship to the person or thing that is the problem. For example, food is not evil. However, if we have such a distorted relationship to food that we gain 100 pounds a year, that is what is the problem, not the food itself. In other words, the food is morally neutral. Likewise, if we are so attached to a human being that we are willing to be manipulated and treated badly by that human being, it is the relationship that must be ended.

Detachment, however, is not a quality that people should seek for its own sake. Detachment is not a goal; it is a strategy to get to a goal. The purpose of detachment is to prevent people or things from blocking our paths to God. In other words, detachment helps us to treasure the things of this world—especially people—but not become so in love with them that we forget that God is to always be number one in our lives. God must always be our number one priority. Everything else is secondary. By becoming detached from people or things, we become liberated or free to give our hearts to God more fully.

One man who understood this very well was a man named Bill Wilson. Bill was a stock broker from New York City who was an alcoholic. Though he tried to break free from his alcoholism, he failed. Then one day, while a patient at Towns Hospital, Bill had a conversion experience. In a fit of despair, Bill cried out, "I'll do anything! Anything at all! If there is a God, let Him show himself." Bill reports that as soon as he said this, he experienced a sensation of bright light, tremendous peace and a feeling of ecstasy. He never drank again.

Soon afterwards, he met people from the Oxford Group. There he learned some solid spiritual principles and tried to help other alcoholics keep sober. He failed at helping others, but in sharing his story with suffering alcoholics, he found that he was able to keep himself sober.

On May 12, 1935, Bill was on a business trip to Akron, Ohio. Desperate to find another alcoholic to help, he called several churches before he found one that referred him to an alcoholic physician by the name of Bob Smith. Bob invited Bill to his house and said he'd give Bill "a minute" to pitch whatever it was he was selling. The "minute" became hours. The two men connected in a most amazing way. What developed from this meeting in Akron, Ohio, became known as what many hold to be the most dynamic spiritual happening of the 20th Century, Alcoholics Anonymous. The first group that called itself "Alcoholics Anonymous" met in my hometown, Cleveland, Ohio. Eventually, Alcoholics Anonymous spread throughout the world, and people who had tried to become free from alcohol by other means now found they could through this spiritual program. Soon, other organizations based on this 12-step spirituality formed, groups such as Overeaters Anonymous, Al-Anon, Codependents Anonymous and many others.

The final goal of AA is to help people have a good life, a life that they cannot have without liberating themselves from alcohol. Like the alcoholic who must get rid of alcohol that is an obstacle in his or her life, we must find those obstacles in our lives that we need to remove to be truly free to follow Christ. Perhaps this obstacle is a person who leads us into temptation or hurts us. Maybe it is a habit that is destroying our spiritual path such as overspending. Or maybe we simply need to avoid a thing entirely so that we never have to worry about having a problem, such as avoiding casinos and other places where we may become addicted to gambling.

As we continue our life journeys this week, it would be a good idea to look at our own lives. What kinds of obstacles do we have on our spiritual paths that prevent us from putting God first? How can we eliminate these obstacles?

And that is the good news I have for you on this 23rd Sunday in Ordinary Time.

Chapter 47

24th Sunday in Ordinary Time - C
Lincoln: Lost & Found

Scripture:

- Exodus 32: 7-11, 13-14
- Psalm 51: 3-4, 12-13, 17 & 19
- 1 Timothy 1: 12-17
- Luke 15: 1-32

Today, Catholic Christians celebrate the 24th Sunday in Ordinary Time. On this day, we hear three stories from Jesus in the Gospel of Luke. These stories are called "lost-and-found" types of stories. In each story, we see someone lose something very special—a coin, a sheep and a son. The good news of the story, however, is that each lost thing was found, and this led to rejoicing.

In the Catholic Christian worldview, our focus is always on goodness and light, not on the evil and darkness that we sometimes encounter in this world.

In this world, each of us experiences losses. Some of the things we lose include loved ones or careers or health or houses or dreams. Sometimes, the thing we lose is our own value system and we go astray. Fortunately, however, we are called to persevere in our life journeys. We are called to seek a better day. We are called to grow. If one door is closed in our face, we search for another that is open to us. We are called to not give up.

The following story shows how one man, one of the greatest Americans who ever lived, continually lost but never gave up. As a result of his persistence, he made a profound imprint on this nation, making it a much better place.

Abraham Lincoln was born in a one-room log cabin in Kentucky on February 12, 1809. Though he was raised in poverty, he had a profound love of knowledge. All through his life, he experienced defeat as a politician and a businessman and suffered from severe depression, but he didn't quit. And because he didn't quit, he became the 16th president of the United States. Most people would agree that of all American presidents, Abraham Lincoln stands out as one of the greatest, if not the greatest.

In 1816, when he around 9 years old, Lincoln's family was forced out of their home and he had to work to help support them. Two years later, his mother died. In 1831, his business failed. In 1832, he ran for state legislature in Illinois but lost the election. In the same year, he also lost his job and was not able to get into law school as he wanted.

In 1833, he borrowed some money from a friend to begin a new business, but by the end of the year he was bankrupt. It took him 17 years to pay off this debt.

In 1834, he again ran for the state legislature in Illinois and lost. A year later, he became engaged to marry but his fiancé died, breaking his heart. The following year, in 1836, he had what was called a total nervous breakdown and was bedridden for six months. In 1838, he tried to become the speaker of the state legislature but was defeated, and in 1840, he sought to become an elector but was defeated. In 1843, he ran for the United States Congress but lost.

Finally, in 1846, Abraham Lincoln ran for Congress and won. In Washington, he did a good job representing his State of Illinois, but in 1848, when he ran for re-election, he lost. A year later, he sought the job of land officer in Illinois, but he was rejected. In 1854, Abraham Lincoln ran for Senate of the United States and lost. Two years later, he sought the vice-presidential nomination of his party, but he got less than 100 votes. And in 1856, two years later, he ran again for the United States Senate and lost. But two years later, in 1860, Abraham Lincoln was elected as the 16th president of the United States.

During his term in office, the Civil War in the United States had the free states of the North at war with the slave states of the South. Lincoln's most famous achievement during that time of war was the signing of the Emancipation Proclamation, which ended the evil of slavery in this country.

On April 14, 1865, Good Friday that year, President Lincoln and his wife were at the Ford's Theater in Washington to see a play. During the play, a man named John Wilkes Booth shot and killed President Lincoln, making him the first American president to be assassinated in office. There would be, in time, three other American presidents assassinated in office including the only Catholic president, John F. Kennedy in 1963.

In looking at the life of Abraham Lincoln, we can't help but be amazed by all of the losses he experienced. Instead of allowing the losses to bury him, however, he picked himself up and tried again. For example, after he lost a Senate race, Lincoln said, "The path was worn and slippery. My foot slipped from under me, knocking the other out of the way, but I recovered and said to myself, 'It's a slip and not a fall.'"

In examining the words of Jesus about being lost and found, and in the life of Abraham Lincoln, one critically important thing to remember is that life is a journey composed of a series of events and stages. To judge someone on just one stage in their life would be incredibly wrong. At many times in his life, for example, Abraham Lincoln could have been judged to be "mentally ill" or "a loser." And at various points in his life, those labels could have applied. But for Catholic Christians, we focus on what we can become, not on what we were. Our focus is based on hope and a belief in romantic or "happily ever after" endings. After all, we fully believe that at the end of time, goodness will overcome evil, love will conquer hate, light will dispel darkness, and life will overcome death. That, my friends, is called the Catholic worldview.

As we continue our life journeys this week, it would be a good idea to reflect on our own lives. How many times have we fallen or been lost? How were we found?

And that is the good news I have for you on this 24th Sunday in Ordinary Time.

Story Source: "Abraham Lincoln Didn't Quit." *Chicken Soup for the Soul*, Ed. Jack Canfield & Mark Victor Hansen. 1993, pp. 236-237.

Chapter 48

25th Sunday in Ordinary Time - C
The Lady with the Rose

Scripture:

- Amos 8: 4-7
- Psalm 113: 1-2, 4-6, 7-8
- 1 Timothy 2: 1-8
- Luke 16: 1-13

Today, Catholic Christians celebrate the 25th Sunday in Ordinary Time. On this day, we hear Jesus talk about being trustworthy. He says, in the Gospel of Luke, "The person who is trustworthy in small matters is also trustworthy in great ones; and the person who is dishonest in very small matters is also dishonest in great ones" (Luke 16: 11).

Trustworthiness is a virtue. Persons who are trustworthy are persons of integrity. If they tell you something, you know they are telling you the truth. If they tell you they will show up for an event, you can be sure they will show up unless there is something very serious that prevents them from showing up. If you swear them to secrecy, they will keep the secret. People who are trustworthy are those whose word is their bond. You can place your trust in them.

In today's Gospel selection from Luke, Jesus praises trustworthy, honest persons by giving a story. He assures his listeners that a person who is truly trustworthy is trustworthy in both small and large things.

In the following story by John Blanchard called "The Lady with the Rose," we encounter a young sailor whose integrity was tested. Because he passed the test, he was rewarded greatly.

The story takes place in World War II. A young sailor became a pen pal with a woman that he had never met. The way it happened was that one day, while he was in a library getting a book, he noticed some pencil notes in the margin. He found the notes to be very profound and loving, so he decided then and there that he wanted to meet the person who had written such beautiful thoughts.

The sailor asked the librarian and got the name and address of the woman who had written the notes. The day after he wrote the mystery woman a note of introduction, he was sent overseas. For the next year, the mystery woman and the young sailor corresponded regularly. They each enjoyed sharing themselves with each other, including their deepest thoughts. At different times, the sailor asked the woman to send him her photo, but he never received one. Nevertheless, their feelings for each other grew stronger.

Finally, the sailor came back to the United States from the war. He and his mysterious female pen pal agreed that they would meet at 7 o'clock in the evening at Grand Central Station in New York City. The woman told the sailor that she would wear a red rose in her lapel so that he could recognize her.

Shortly after the sailor arrived at the station, he saw a tall, beautiful blond woman in a pale green suit walk by. The lonely young man was immediately attracted to her and her alluring vitality and sensuality. She smiled at him and said, "Going my way, sailor?" as she passed by.

But her spell over him was broken when he suddenly saw behind her a woman wearing a red rose on her lapel. His heart sank because the woman was as plain as the blonde was stunning. The woman with the rose was overweight, in her late 40s, and had graying hair. But, her eyes sparkled, and she had a gentle face.

As the beautiful blonde in the green dress walked away, the young sailor hesitated for just a moment. He turned his back on the beauty and headed to the simple woman who wore the red rose. As he looked at her, he realized that his fantasies for a romantic relationship would not be realized. On the other hand, he thought, this woman had written such beautiful letters to him over the past year, that perhaps she could become a lifelong friend, a friend whose wit and intelligence he already knew from their correspondence.

When the young sailor got to the middle-aged woman, he introduced himself and suggested that they go out to dinner. But the older woman just smiled at him with amusement and said, "I don't know what this is all about, son, but the young women in the green suit who just went by begged me to wear this rose on my coat. And she said that if you were to ask me out to dinner, she's waiting for you in the restaurant across the street. She said it was some kind of a test."

Needless to say, the young man passed the test. He showed integrity of character. He was trustworthy. And for that, we can only guess that he was well rewarded and lived happily ever after.

Although we may not be tested in such a dramatic and colorful way as the young sailor in this story, you and I are tested each day. We are given many opportunities to show that we are trustworthy in both small and large things. As Christians, we are called to clothe ourselves in a blanket of virtue, among them honesty and trustworthiness. We are called to show up when we say we will, to keep secrets when we say we will, to work when we say we will, and to live our vocations faithfully every day.

As we continue our life journeys this week, it would be a good idea to examine our own lives. How do we show we are trustworthy? How do we fail in this regard?

And that is the good news I have for you on this 25th Sunday in Ordinary Time.

Story Source: Blanchard, John. "The Lady with the Rose." *A World of Stories for Preachers and Teachers*, Ed. William J. Bausch. 1998, #76, pp. 222-223.

Chapter 49

26th Sunday in Ordinary Time - C
Two at the Counter

Scripture:

- Amos 6: 1a, 4-7
- Psalm 146: 6c-7, 8-9a, 9bc-10
- 1 Timothy 6: 11-16
- Luke 16: 19-31

Today, Catholic Christians celebrate the 26th Sunday in Ordinary Time. On this day, we read in St. Paul's First Letter to Timothy some of the qualities that a good Christian should possess. Among these qualities are righteousness, devotion, faith, love, patience and gentleness. Today, we explore the concept of patience, a virtue that is often very difficult to practice in our fast-moving society.

Patience is a virtue that helps people bear suffering over a period of time courageously. Patience is part of a bigger virtue called fortitude, or courage. Patience is something that is easier to talk about than to practice in everyday life. That is what Preacher Pike discovered one day when he went to eat at a diner.

After sitting at a lunch counter, Preacher Pike waited for three minutes. Waitresses passed him by, and two cooks and a busboy didn't even notice him sitting there. The preacher became angrier and angrier. The only thing that made him feel a little better was that a truck driver, who was seated next to him, was equally ignored. Preacher Pike said, "Maybe this counter is off limits." The trucker replied, "Well, maybe they are short of help today."

After a couple more minutes, Preacher Pike angrily said, "Maybe they don't want our business." The trucker responded with, "Maybe they are taking care of those who are seated at the tables."

After a couple more minutes, Preacher Pike, his blood pressure continuing to rise, said, "Maybe they don't like us." The truck driver replied, "The air conditioning feels so good I don't mind waiting."

At this point, a stressed waitress stopped at the counter and apologized to the two men. She explained that the water had been cut off, and the dishwasher was not working. The trucker smiled, thanked the waitress for the explanation, and left. Preacher Pike did not like the trucker, for three times he had tried to get the trucker to back up his obnoxious attitude, but the trucker refused to be brought into negativity. Only then did Preacher Pike realize that the trucker had been patient. The trucker had practiced what Preacher Pike only preached.

As this story shows, preaching about patience is always much easier than practicing patience in everyday life. In celebrating the Sacrament of Reconciliation each week, I find that a lack of patience is one of the most common struggles that people have today. That is quite understandable as we live hectic lifestyles that are filled with so many demands pulling us in too many different directions.

When looking at the virtue of patience, here are three things that we should always remember.

First, almost every spiritual writer strongly advises not to pray for the virtue of patience. They say that because patience, like all other virtues, is perfected with practice. Thus, if you deliberately pray for patience, and if God takes you seriously, God will put all kinds of things in your path that will test you, things like putting painfully slow drivers in front of you on a one-lane road, putting you in the slowest line at the supermarket, having you surrounded by coworkers who don't give you what you need, and the like. Jesus warned us about this very thing when he said, "Therefore, do not worry about tomorrow, for tomorrow will take care of itself. Sufficient for a day is its own evil" (Matthew 6:34). In other words, if we pray for patience, we're just asking for it. We're asking God to shower us with patience-testing opportunities when, in reality, we already have more than enough opportunities in everyday life.

Second, whenever possible, we should try to prevent occasions that normally lead us to impatience. The great American Benjamin Franklin advocated that when he said, "An ounce of prevention is worth a pound of cure." Not only is this a very wise dictum for physical health, it is a wise dictum for spiritual and mental health.

There are many practical ways of avoiding impatience-causing events. For example, when we wait until the last minute to do things, we tend to get frustrated when the rest of the world seems to be in slow motion. If we allowed ourselves more time, we would not be so frazzled. We can also turn impatience-producing events into something more enjoyable. For example, it is very frustrating to wait in a physician's office if we have nothing to do but get angry about waiting. Therefore, we can take a good book with us so that the time flies by. Avoiding substances such as caffeine can also help if we have a problem with patience. We can go shopping or to an ATM machine when traffic is lighter rather than going during rush hour. And of course, we can steel our resolve when we know we will be encountering people or events that tend to push our buttons.

And third, we should remember to thank God when we are successful in demonstrating the virtue of patience. This is part of living an examined life. When we live such a life, we are aware of our little triumphs, and after each triumph, we thank God for helping us to achieve them. After all, it is only with God's grace that we make breakthroughs in our spiritual journeys.

As we continue our life journeys this week, it would be a good idea to examine our own lives. What are the people, places or things that lead us to impatience? What type of strategies can we employ to lessen our chances of being impatient?

That is the good news I have for you on this 26th Sunday in Ordinary Time.

Story Source: Pike, Jr., Rev. Martin E. "Two at the Counter." *A World of Stories for Preachers & Teachers*, Ed. William J. Bausch. 1998, #249. p. 350.

Chapter 50

27th Sunday in Ordinary Time - C
Fr. Emil Kapaun

Scripture:

- Habakkuk 1: 2-3; 2: 2-4
- Psalm 95: 1-2, 6-7c, 7d-9
- 2 Timothy 1: 6-8,13-14
- Luke 17: 5-10

Today, Catholic Christians celebrate the 27th Sunday in Ordinary Time, which is also known as Respect Life Sunday, a day dedicated to the idea that all people are to be treated with dignity and respect as children of God.

On this day, we read in the Second Letter to Timothy that following Jesus is not always easy. On the contrary, it is often fraught with hardship. Paul says, "...bear your share of hardship for the gospel with the strength that comes from God" (2 Timothy 1:8).

Although all of us are called to follow this advice, some are called to do so in the most remarkable of ways. One man who was called to share hardship for the gospel in an extraordinary way was an American priest from the Diocese of Wichita, Kansas, Fr. Emil Kapaun.

Emil was born on April 16, 1916 near Pilsen, Kansas of Bohemian immigrant parents.

In 1940, Emil was ordained a priest for the Diocese of Wichita, Kansas and celebrated his first Mass of Thanksgiving at St. John Nepomucene in Pilsen, Kansas. In December 1943, he was appointed pastor of that parish.

Though he came from the same Bohemian heritage as many of the congregation, many of the Bohemian members of the parish did not like him too much. They knew him as a child, and it was hard for them to see him as their priest. Plus, Fr. Emil was not too happy being in a comfortable parish setting when he felt there was much more he should be doing for the Lord.

In October 1944, Fr. Kapaun became a chaplain in the United States Army. With one other chaplain, he ministered to 19,000 servicemen and women. Later, he served in India and Burma and was promoted to captain in January 1946. In May 1946, he returned to the United States and was discharged from the Army. He then earned a Master of Arts degree in education at The Catholic University of America in Washington, D.C. in 1948.

In September 1948, Fr. Kapaun re-enlisted in the U.S. Army as a military chaplain and left the United States in December 1949, never to return. After serving in Japan, he was sent to Korea, a month after North Korea had invaded South Korea. Fr. Kapaun found himself in the thick of battles. Continually, he served the men by celebrating Mass with the altar being the front end of a jeep, hearing confessions, baptizing others, caring for the sick and injured, and constantly encouraging the men.

In November 1950, Fr. Kapaun refused to leave some men who were injured in battle. As a result, he was captured by the North Korean soldiers. He and other prisoners of war were marched 87 miles to a prison camp near Pyoktong, North Korea. In the camp, Fr. Kapaun continually encouraged his fellow prisoners not to give up hope. He dug latrines, gave away his meager food to others, and picked lice off the prisoners who were too sick to do it for themselves.

One of the things Fr. Kapaun was most noted for was his great ability to steal food for those who were hungry. In fact, a television movie that was made about him in 1955 was called "The Good Thief."

Fr. Kapaun encouraged the men with prayer, good words, Scripture and a healthy sense of humor. At times, he was brutally punished for disobeying orders from his captors. Sometimes, for example, he would be forced to spend the night sitting naked in subzero weather.

When his Communist captors forced him into a mandatory re-education camp, Fr. Kapaun calmly rejected every theory they put to him. His Communist captors, knowing of his tremendous influence over other prisoners, were very afraid of him.

When the Chinese overtook the area, they were a little bit more lenient with the prisoners than the North Koreans had been. But Fr. Kapaun developed a blood clot in his leg in 1951. That, coupled with dysentery and pneumonia, made him weaker and weaker. Finally, the Chinese moved him to a hospital where he died of pneumonia on May 23, 1951. He was buried in a mass grave near the Yalu River.

Stories about Fr. Kapaun's incredible heroism and powerful influence on the men began to be told overseas and in this country. Soon, hospitals and schools and military buildings and chapels and Knights of Columbus councils began to be named after him.

In 1993, Emil Kapaun was named "Servant of God" by the Catholic Church, the first step in the process of canonization.

On April 11, 2013, President Barack Obama presented the United States' highest military decoration—the Medal of Honor—to Fr. Kapaun's nephew, Ray Kapaun. As President Obama said, "This is an amazing story. Father Kapaun has been called a shepherd in combat boots.

His fellow soldiers who felt his grace and his mercy called him a saint, a blessing from God. Today, we bestow another title on him – recipient of our nation's highest military decoration."

President Obama noted, as Fr. Kapaun's military captors were sending him to isolation without food or water to die, Fr. Kapaun looked at the guards and said, "Forgive them, for they know not what they do."

As we continue our life journeys this week, it would be a good idea to reflect on our commitment to the Faith. Would we be as brave as Servant of God Emil Kapaun if we were called to suffer for the Faith?

And that is the good news I have for you on this 27th Sunday in Ordinary Time.

Story Sources:

"Emil Kapaun: Wikipedia, the free encyclopedia.

"President Obama Awards Medal of Honor to Father Emil Kapaun" – White House Blog, April 11, 2013.

Chapter 51

28th Sunday in Ordinary Time - C
When You Thought I Wasn't Looking

Scripture:

- 2 Kings 5: 14-17
- Psalm 98: 1, 2-3ab, 3cd-4
- 2 Timothy 2: 8-13
- Luke 17: 11-19

Today, Catholic Christians celebrate the Twenty-Eighth Sunday in Ordinary Time. On this day, we hear one of the most famous stories in the Bible that discusses the concept of thanksgiving, that of the ten lepers.

In this story, ten lepers were cured by Jesus. As you may remember, leprosy was considered to be an incurable disease at the time, and lepers were isolated from the rest of society. So to be cured of this most terrible disease was a most amazing thing. But in this story, the only person who returned to say "thank you" to Jesus was a Samaritan man. As you may remember, the Jews of Jesus' time despised Samaritans, so this story must have made the Jewish listeners very uncomfortable, if not downright angry. It would be like telling a story today with Jesus curing ten people with terminal cancer, nine of them being Catholic Christians and one of them being a Muslim. If only the Muslim came back to thank Jesus for this miracle, I think we Catholic Christians would not be very happy with the story.

From the time we are little, our parents and teachers encouraged us to be thankful for all of our blessings. Especially, we were encouraged to thank God for our parents and pets and friends. But if we truly examine our lives and the magnificent world in which we live, the list of what we should be grateful for would be endless. That is what we see in the following essay by a woman named Mary Rita Schilke Korazan. It is called "When You Thought I Wasn't Looking."

> When you thought I wasn't looking I saw you hang
>   my first painting on the refrigerator, and I immediately
>   wanted to paint another one.
> When you thought I wasn't looking I saw you feed
>   a stray cat, and I learned that it was good to be kind
>   to animals.
> When you thought I wasn't looking I saw you make
>   my favorite cake for me, and I learned that the little
>   things can be the special things in life.
> When you thought I wasn't looking I heard you say
>   a prayer, and I knew that there is a God I could always
>   talk to, and I learned to trust in Him.
> When you thought I wasn't looking I saw you make

a meal and take it to a friend who was sick, and I
learned that we all have to help take care of each other.
When you thought I wasn't looking, I saw you give
of your time and money to help people who had
nothing, and I learned that those who have something
should give to those who don't.
When you thought I wasn't looking I saw you take
care of our house and everyone in it, and I learned we
have to take care of what we are given.
When you thought I wasn't looking I saw how you
handled your responsibilities, even when you didn't
feel good, and I learned that I would have to be
responsible when I grow up.
When you thought I wasn't looking I saw tears
come from your eyes, and I learned that sometimes
things hurt, but it's all right to cry.
When you thought I wasn't looking I saw that you
cared, and I wanted to be everything that I could be.
When you thought I wasn't looking I learned most
of life's lessons that I need to know to be a good and
productive person when I grow up.
When you thought I wasn't looking, I looked at you
and wanted to say, 'Thanks for all the things I saw
when you thought I wasn't looking.'

This essay is relevant for all of us today, for it shows us so many things
that we take for granted, things for which we should be thankful.

Having hearts of gratitude is not only something God wants for us,
but is essential to our mental, spiritual, and physical well-being. Scientific
research shows that grateful people are more mentally healthy, and this
translates into good physical and spiritual health. It is only when we
begin to focus on what we don't have that we get ourselves into trouble.

As we continue our life journeys this week, it would be a good idea to
reflect on our own lives. Do we focus on what we have instead of what we
don't have? Do we show our gratitude by sharing abundantly with others?
Do we remember to thank God every day for all of our blessings?

And that is the good news I have for you on this Twenty-Eighth Sunday in Ordinary Time.

Story Source: "When You Thought I Wasn't Looking" by Mary Rita Schilke Korazan, found in several internet sources.

Chapter 52

29th Sunday in Ordinary Time - C
Tutu & Perserverance

Scripture:

- Exodus 17: 8-13
- Psalm 121: 1-2, 3-4, 5-6, 7-8
- 2 Timothy 3: 14 – 4: 2
- Luke 18: 1-8

Today, Catholic Christians celebrate the 29th Sunday in Ordinary Time. Throughout the world, we celebrate this as World Mission Sunday, a day we are challenged to give to further the work of Catholic missionaries throughout the world.

In the Gospel of Luke, we read the story of a widow who wanted a judge to render a just decision for her. Unfortunately, the judge was not good, and he continued to ignore her. The widow, however, continued to persist in her quest. Finally, the judge gave in and granted her request to make her quit bothering him.

This story is about persistence, and persistence is related to the virtue of perseverance. Persistence refers to doing something over and over again until one gets one's way. Sometimes, persistence has a negative tone, as in the bill collector persistently calling until she got payment. Perseverance, on the other hand, is usually always seen as good. It refers to having the will to see things through until the end in spite of obstacles or fears or discouragement. Perseverance, in Catholic Christian thought, is seen as a virtue.

In the following story, we see how one man's perseverance led a whole nation to change for the better. The man's name is Desmond Tutu.

Desmond Tutu lived in South Africa at a time when apartheid existed. Apartheid was a system of legal racial segregation. Blacks were considered inferior under the law and treated accordingly. That is the society in which Desmond, a black African, grew up and became a teacher and later a priest.

After Desmond Tutu became an Anglican priest, he studied in London. He was shocked at the freedom he experienced there. No longer did he fear that every police officer was a potential enemy, empowered to detain any black person for whatever reason. In fact, Tutu was amazed that the police were actually polite to him. Sometimes, Tutu walked the streets of London at night just to have the pleasure of not being arrested. He was surprised that people could speak in Hyde Park on any subject, no matter how outrageous, and be protected by the authorities.

One time, when Fr. Tutu was waiting in line at the bank, a white man cut in front of him. The bank teller told the white man to wait his turn. Tutu was astonished at this, for such an act of justice would be unheard of in his native South Africa.

When he returned to South Africa, Fr. Tutu began a long and often painful battle for equality for his people. For the next three decades, he struggled against the racist government of South Africa. Often, however, he found himself struggling against those who believed that the only way for racial equality in the nation was through violence. Fr. Tutu, who became the first Anglican archbishop in the country in 1985, was frequently the target of arrests, death threats and slander. He often risked his life to save those of his own people from mobs who thought they were government spies.

Through his nonviolent presence and consistent preaching, hope for a better tomorrow began to spread among the black population of South Africa. In February of 1988, Archbishop Tutu and fellow ministers gathered at a cathedral in Cape Town. There, they prayed and began a march for freedom. They didn't get very far, however, for the police arrested them and charged them as criminals.

Soon after being arrested, Archbishop Tutu prophesied in a sermon:

> We must say to our rulers, especially unjust rulers such as those in this land, "You may be powerful, indeed very powerful. But you are not God. You are ordinary mortals! God—the God whom we worship—can't be mocked. You have already lost! You have already lost! Let us say to you nicely: 'You have already lost, we are inviting you to come and join the winning side.'"

Five years later, black South Africans voted in their first national election. In front of a crowd of 70,000 people, Archbishop Tutu introduced South Africa's first black president, Nelson Mandela.

Because of his persistence and perseverance, and with the grace of God, Desmond Tutu was able to do God's will in his life. He was able to be an apostle of equality.

We, too, need to strive to do God's will in our lives, and we need both persistence and perseverance. But when we practice these, we need to keep three things in mind:

First, be sure what you are fighting for is worthy. Sometimes, people go off on tangents, spending all their energy on things that are not really important. If you are going to spend your life fighting for something, be sure it is something very important.

Second, persistence and perseverance do not trump virtues such as charity. Desmond Tutu remembered that. That is why he always put the virtue of love first and foremost in all his actions. In Catholic Christianity, we call this, "Charity in all things."

And third, when we fight for something good, we need to keep a Catholic worldview in mind when things get tough. In other words, we need to remember that in the end, good will overcome evil, light will dispel darkness and love will overcome hate.

As we continue our life journeys this week, it would be a good idea to reflect on our own lives. How do we show perseverance in our lives?

And that is the good news I have for you on this 29th Sunday in Ordinary Time.

Story Source: Temple, Todd. "Oh God, How Long." *Still More Hot Illustrations for Youth Talks*, Ed. Wayne Rice. 1999, pp. 113-114.

Chapter 53

30th Sunday in Ordinary Time - C
Carjacking Foiled

Scripture:

- Sirach 35: 12-14, 16-18
- Psalm 34: 2-3, 17-18, 19 & 23
- 2 Timothy 4: 6-8, 16-18
- Luke 18: 9-14

Today, Catholic Christians celebrate the 30th Sunday in Ordinary Time. On this day, we hear Jesus tell one of his "good guy-bad guy" types of stories. In the story, two men went to the temple to pray. One of them was a Pharisee, a member of the Jewish people who were supposed to be very holy. The other man was a tax collector, someone whom the Jews looked down as a traitor. The Pharisee was arrogant, judging himself to be holier than others. The tax collector, however, showed humility and asked God to forgive him. In the story, Jesus said that the tax collector was the one who was justified, not the Pharisee.

In Catholic Christian theology, to be justified means that a human being, through a gracious act of God, is made holy and endowed with grace. Thus, in this story, the Pharisee was the bad guy while the tax collector was the good guy.

One of the main morals of this story is that we should not judge ourselves to be morally superior to others or to judge others to be inferior in holiness than ourselves. Absolutely none of us knows the state of another person's soul. Only God can know how holy or unholy a person is. Unfortunately, however, sometimes we look at others and judge them. This is not only condemned by Jesus, it is also a dangerous practice because we make errors based on rash judgments. That is exactly what happened to an elderly woman in the following story.

There was once an elderly woman in California who was a rather feisty person. She was known for taking care of herself and not letting anything or anyone get in her way. One day, she went to the supermarket to do grocery shopping. When she returned to her car, she noticed four men getting into it.

The woman dropped her shopping bags, reached into her purse, and pulled out a gun that she always carried for protection. She ran in front of the car and aimed her pistol at the men. She then began screaming for the men to get out of the car or she would blow their brains out.

She screamed, "I know how to use this gun, and don't think I won't!"

The four men, scared out of their wits, threw open the car doors and ran as fast as they could away from her.

The woman was trembling, but she tried to keep calm. When she was certain the men were gone, she put her gun back into her purse, picked up her groceries, and loaded the bags in her car. She then got into the driver's seat to start her car so that she could go to the police station to report that four men had tried to steal her car. There was one problem, however: her key did not fit into the ignition. She glanced around the inside of the car and discovered, to her horror that she was in the wrong car. Her car, which looked like the one she had entered, was parked a few spaces away.

She then loaded the bags of groceries from the wrong car to her car and drove to the police station to confess to what had happened. When she told the story to the sergeant, he couldn't stop laughing. He just pointed to the other end of the counter where four very shaken men were reporting a carjacking by a mad, elderly woman.

The woman apologized, and nobody was charged with a crime.

This is a wonderful story, for it shows how even well-intentioned people can make serious errors in judging others. And when we do that, we are violating the Christian commandment not to judge others.

When we judge others, we are engaging in self-righteousness. Self-righteousness is the belief that one is morally superior to others. This defect is also known as being sanctimonious or holier-than-thou. This spiritual disorder is deadly for many reasons. Here are just three:

First, as mentioned earlier, no one can know the state of another person's soul. There may be tens of thousands of prisoners in the United States who are much holier than a person who attends daily Mass. Although we may guess about how holy or unholy a person is, it is merely a guess. When we look at the lives of the saints, for example, we see some pretty wild characters. The very first saint of the Church was the good thief, the man killed by capital punishment who Jesus told would be with him that day in paradise.

Second, judging others or being self-righteous is spiritual egotism, a form of pride. And we know pride is the deadliest of all vices. Like a deadly disease, pride can infect the entire moral system of a human soul.

And third, frequently self-righteousness leads to acts against charity, the highest of all virtues and the greatest commandment of Jesus Christ. Judging others to be morally inferior to us can lead to such things as treating them with less respect than others, denying them rights, or shunning them from our circle of friends. In other words, self-righteousness can lead us to fail to treat others as we would treat Jesus Christ who lives in all people.

As we continue our life journeys this week, it would be a good idea to examine our own lives. How often do we fall into the sin of judging others to be morally inferior to ourselves? What do we do to correct this failing?

And that is the good news I have for you on this 30th Sunday in Ordinary Time.

Story Source: "Car Jacking Foiled." *Hot Illustrations for Youth Talks 4*, Ed. Wayne Rice. 2001, pp. 26-27.

Chapter 54

31ˢᵗ Sunday in Ordinary Time - C
I Know You

Scripture:

- Wisdom 11: 22 – 12: 2
- Psalm 145: 1-2, 8-9, 10-11, 13cd-14
- 2 Thessalonians 1: 11- 2: 2
- Luke 19: 1-10

Today, Catholic Christians celebrate the 31ˢᵗ Sunday in Ordinary Time. On this day, we hear the story of Zacchaeus, the chief tax collector of a town who was very wealthy. When he heard that Jesus would be passing through town, he was very excited. The crowds around Jesus were large, and Zacchaeus was very small. Therefore, he climbed a sycamore tree so he could get a glimpse of Jesus.

Imagine how surprised and proud and thrilled Zacchaeus must have been when Jesus looked up at him in the tree and said, "Zacchaeus, come down quickly, for today I must stay at your house."

The other people were very jealous and grumbled that Jesus was eating with someone they considered a sinner. Note that they didn't see themselves as sinners, only the tax collector. They were filled with pride and arrogance.

At the house, however, Zacchaeus told Jesus all the good he would do for the people and Jesus was very pleased and told the tax collector, "Today salvation has come to this house..."

It is now 2,000 years later, and people still sit in judgment of others. They still look down on those they feel are morally inferior. They still like to see themselves as better than others. They seem to never learn.

Each one of us knows, however, that if others truly knew all there is to know about us, we would be ashamed. If they knew our thoughts and bad things we have done in the past, we would be mortified. None of us is without sin. That is what we see in the following story of a judge who understood this all too clearly. Though the author of the story is unknown, it was printed by Wayne Rice.

There was once a small town that held a trial. It was the kind of town where everybody knew everybody else's business. The whole town showed up for the trial. The prosecuting attorney called his first witness, an elderly woman, to the stand. He walked up to her and asked, "Mrs. Jones, do you know me?"

Mrs. Jones replied, "Of course I know you, Mr. Williams. I've know you since you were a little boy. And to tell you the truth, you have been a great disappointment to me. You lie, you cheat on your wife, you manipulate people and you talk behind their backs. You think you are a rising star in your field, but you don't have the brains to amount to anything important in life. You're nothing more than a paper-pusher. Yes, I sure do know you."

The prosecuting attorney was stunned. Not knowing what else to do, he pointed across the room and asked, "Mrs. Jones, do you know the defense attorney?"

She replied, "Well, of course I do. I've known Mr. Bradley since he was a little boy also. I used to babysit him. And he, too, has been a real disappointment to me. Besides having a drinking problem, he is lazy and bigoted. He can't build a normal relationship with anyone. His law practice is one of the shoddiest in the entire state. I can't imagine why they even let him practice law. Yes, I know him."

At this point, the judge rapped the courtroom to silence and called both the prosecuting attorney and defense attorney to his bench.

Covering up his microphone, he said with menace in a very quiet voice, "If either of you asks her if she knows me, I'll hold you both in contempt of court!"

The judge was wise. He knew something that many people never fully realize. That something he knew was that every human being is human. Every one of us shares the same struggles and dreams and fantasies and faults and hopes and visions.

I know a man who was an archabbot, the head of an archabbey. After he had been in his position for quite some time, someone asked him what he had learned. He smiled and said, "After listening to and observing the other monks for a long time, I have come to the amazing realization that we are all the same. We all have gifts and challenges and sins and faults and quirks and joys and dreams and visions. Though we all have different names and different histories, basically, we are all the same."

Jesus, who was both God and man, knew this very profound truth. He was able to see the goodness in Zacchaeus' heart even though others could not see it. Jesus could also see the faults in the thoughts and hearts of Zacchaeus' neighbors. So, although the neighbors were amazed that Jesus chose the tax collector to dine with, we should not be surprised. Jesus is, after all, for everyone, not just those who have a high opinion of themselves and look down on others.

From the Gospel story and from the story of the woman who knew too much, we should remember that judging others is wrong. To see ourselves as morally superior to others is wrong.

As we continue our life journeys this week, it would be a good idea to reflect on this question: How am I basically just like other human beings?

And that is the good news I have for you on this 31ˢᵗ Sunday in Ordinary Time.

Story Source: "I Know You." *How Illustrations for Youth Talks 4*, Ed. Wayne Rice. 2001, pp. 112-113.

Chapter 55

32nd Sunday in Ordinary Time - C
The Four Chaplains

Scripture:

- 2 Maccabees 7: 1-2, 9-14
- Psalm 17: 1, 5-6, 8 & 15
- 2 Thessalonians 2: 16 – 3: 5
- Luke 20: 27-38

Today, Catholic Christians celebrate the 32nd Sunday in Ordinary Time. In just three more weeks, the Church year will come to an end, and we'll enter a brand new Church year. The Scripture readings reflect this reality as they become more and more focused on life in heaven.

This Sunday, we read a very interesting Old Testament story about a mother and her seven sons. Because they refused to violate the laws of their Jewish religion, the king had them tortured and killed. But as they were tortured, they focused on the world to come, the world where they would spend everlasting peace and joy.

Today, we still have people who give their lives either in service to others or to the Lord as martyrs. That is what we see in the lives of four men who gave their lives in 1943 so that others could live.

The story takes place during World War II on board a ship called the USAT *Dorchester*. Four relatively new chaplains, all of them first lieutenants, served the people on the ship. They were: Rev. George L. Fox, a Methodist minister from Pennsylvania; Rabbi Alexander D. Goode, a Reform Jewish rabbi from Brooklyn, New York; Rev. Clark V. Poling, a minister of the Reformed Church in America from Ohio; and Father John P. Washington, a Roman Catholic priest from Newark, New Jersey.

The *Dorchester* set sail from New York City on January 23, 1943 to Greenland with the four chaplains and about 900 other men, both military and non-military. During the early morning hours of February 3, 1943, a German submarine torpedoed the *Dorchester* off of Newfoundland in the North Atlantic.

The torpedo knocked out the *Dorchester's* electrical system, leaving the ship in darkness. Panic broke out among the men. The four chaplains tried to calm the men and organize an orderly evacuation of the ship. They guided many men to safety. When it became clear that there were not enough life jackets for everyone, the four chaplains took off theirs and gave them to other men.

As a result of the assistance of the chaplains, about 230 of the 904 men on the ship were saved.

One man, as he swam away from the ship, looked back. He reported that the flares had lit up the ship. The last thing he saw were the four chaplains standing together, praying for the safety of the men. The chaplains, who went down with the ship, are often known as "The Four Chaplains" or the "Immortal Chaplains."

Now, when we hear such stories of remarkable heroism, we are justifiably inspired. We also wonder if we would be able to do such remarkable things if we were put in such circumstances.

One thing we often forget, however, is people don't just suddenly have courage to cope with amazing tests. On the contrary, when we look at the lives of martyrs and those who give their lives for others, we see a certain life pattern. St. Paul speaks of this today in his second letter to the Thessalonians. He asked others to pray for him and his fellow ministers so that they could not only continue to spread the good news of Jesus, but that they would be delivered from people who were wicked. He knew that prayer was the fuel that gave them the zeal and courage do their Christian ministry. He knew that what he and his fellow ministers were called to do did not exist in a vacuum. We, likewise, don't do great things as a spur-of-the-moment thing without having an inner core of strength. That strength or grace comes from prayer and living a particular way of life.

One of the four chaplains, Rev. Clark Poling, knew this, and this knowledge is reflected in the last conversation he had with his father, Dr. Dan Poling. Just before Clark reported to the ship that would carry him to his death, he and his dad talked. Clark said, "Dad, remember me as I return to my post of duty."

Dr. Poling replied, "Son, I'll pray every day that God will bring you back home without a scratch."

The young chaplain replied, "No, Dad, don't do that. Don't pray that way. I want you to pray that I will be adequate for any situation."

Needless to say, Clark was adequate for the situation. He gave his life so that another man could live.

Every day, we need the inner strength to meet the challenges of the day. Though we most likely won't be called upon to be killed for the faith or give up our lives so that others might live, we will be called upon to show our Christian identity. We will be called upon to show compassion to those who are suffering. We will be called on to deal charitably with angry and disagreeable people. We will be called upon to exercise patience with others who get on our nerves. We will be called on to not judge those who are not doing their work satisfactorily. We will be called in many,

many ways to show our Christian self. Therefore, we need to live a prayer-centered life in Christ each day.

As we continue our life journey this week, it would be a good idea to reflect on how we live a Christ-centered life of prayer and action that prepares us for anything God will call us to do, no matter how profound or scary.

And that is the good news I have for you on this 32nd Sunday in Ordinary Time.

Story Sources:

"Dad, Remember Me." *Sower's Seeds of Encouragement: Fifth Planting*, Ed. Brian Cavanaugh. 1998, #77, p. 72.

"Four Chaplains." Wikipedia.

Chapter 56

33rd Sunday in Ordinary Time - C
The Happy Hypocrite

Scripture:

- Malachi 3: 19-20a
- Psalm 98: 5-6, 7-9a, 9bc
- 2 Thessalonians 3: 7-12
- Luke 21: 5-19

Today, Catholic Christians celebrate the 33rd Sunday in Ordinary Time. On this day, we encounter a very interesting and practical reading from St. Paul in his second letter to the Thessalonians. In this document, he talks about a recent visit he and his disciples had among the Thessalonians. He noted that he and his followers worked very hard and ate their own food. They did not want to be a burden to their guests. They did that, Paul notes, to be models to the Thessalonians.

Paul went on to say that he had learned that some of the Thessalonians were acting in disorderly ways, being busybodies instead of being hard workers and minding their own business. What Paul was trying to say was that he and his followers were trying to imitate Jesus, to be models that others could follow.

We, too, are called to be imitators of Christ. We, too, are called to practice the virtues Jesus taught such as compassion, mercy, love, hope, faith, patience, courage and others.

Sometimes, though, we just don't feel like imitating Christ. We feel like acting in un-Christian-like ways. But Paul was not discussing feelings – he was discussing behavior. Our Christian call does not depend on our feeling states which come and go. It depends on action. Every adult, for example, knows this. All adults, for example, at one time or another don't feel like going to work, but they do. They do so because that is their job. They put their values ahead of their feelings.

Sometimes, in following Christ, we need to act contrary to our feeling state. In time, our actions can actually change our basic selves. Before discussing this phenomenon in detail, let's look at a very intriguing story called "The Happy Hypocrite."

There was once a man who was born with a very terrible facial deformity. As he grew up, he found that he was lonely, for other people did not want to be around him. When he became an adult, he decided to move away from his hometown to begin a new life. On the way to the new town, he discovered a beautiful mask that fit his face, making him look very handsome. At first, he was uncomfortable with the mask, for he thought people would discover his true self and realize that he was just wearing a mask. But, he continued wearing the mask every day.

Now as we all know, people are attracted to handsome people. In his new town, he made many friends and fell in love. But one day, a wicked woman from his hometown came to the man's new town and discovered the man's true identity. In front of all the man's friends and fiancé, she forced him to remove the mask. When he removed the mask, it revealed a handsome face. Through time, his face became conformed to the mask he had been wearing.

Now, this story might seem far-fetched. We may think, "Well, such a thing could not happen."

Well, I am here to tell you, that it happens every day. True, a mask might not change a person's physical makeup, but we all wear masks every day that can change us in dramatic and positive ways.

Perhaps the best example of this occurs when we enter the "real world" of our occupations. When we are in school studying for a profession, we are coddled and protected. We learn in sheltered environments. Then, when we are thrown out into the real world, we often feel like frauds. But, we put on our professional mask and try to do the best we can even though we feel totally over our head. In our society, we even have a slogan for this: "Fake it till you make it."

As seminarians, for example, we had not even one minute of education in finance, budget-making, fundraising and the like. But as parish priests, we suddenly are expected to conduct capital campaigns to raise millions of dollars and run a parish with a couple of million dollars coming in and going out each year. On top of that, we are expected to hire and fire staff and do a myriad of things we were not taught.

We get a whole semester to design three little homilies, and then as priests we are expected to design one every seven days, rain or shine, and then deliver it in front of a couple thousand people. We fake it till we make it.

That, of course, is true in any profession. Eventually, when we fake it for long enough, we realize one day that we are no longer "faking it." The training wheels have fallen off our bicycles, and we are genuinely riding the big-boy's bike alone. We've arrived!

Imitating Christ is like that. We may not feel like being generous, or forgiving, or patient, or courageous, or honest or whatever on a particular day. So what! Who cares! Imitating Christ is not about feeling states; it is about basing our actions on our Christian values and beliefs. If we imitate Christ long enough, it eventually becomes part of the very fabric of our very being. Then, we can say, we've arrived.

So, as we continue our life journeys this week, it would be good to take some time to reflect on our lives. How do we "fake it till we make it" in our lives? How does this lead to solid performance in our adult social roles and our imitation of Christ?

And that is the good news that I have for you on this 33rd Sunday in Ordinary Time.

Story Source: "The Happy Hypocrite: A Fairy Tale for Tired Men" by Max Beerbohm was published first in 1897 and can be found on Wikipedia, 2014.

Chapter 57

Christ the King - C
Serving Thanksgiving

Scripture:

- 2 Samuel 5: 1-3
- Psalm 122: 1-2, 3-4ab, 4cd-5
- Colossians 1: 12-20
- Luke 23: 35-43

Today, Catholic Christians celebrate The Feast of Christ the King, the last Sunday of the Church year.

Pope Pius XI established this feast in 1925 to honor the idea that Jesus Christ is king of the entire universe, including all nations on earth. In particular, the feast reminds us that Jesus redeemed us all by dying on the cross for us.

Although we probably have no problem with the idea of "Christ the King," we sometimes forget that Jesus is the head of the Catholic Church. In today's Letter of St. Paul to the Colossians, for example, Paul says about Jesus: "He is the head of the body, the Church" (Colossians 1: 18a).

Throughout the more than 2,000 years of the Catholic Church, there have been many people who forgot that Jesus was the head of the Church. They began to confuse teachings of religious leaders with the teachings of Jesus. They became mesmerized by fancy titles of such figures, and they put too much faith in these people. In time, they didn't even question the teachings of the earthly religious leaders to see how these teachings stacked up with the triple love commandment of Jesus: to love God, to love others, as we love ourselves.

Knowing that religious leaders can lead us astray, it is good to always remember that Jesus is the head of the Church. It is his love ethic that should be the center of our moral compass. Following Jesus is not that complicated. On the contrary, it can be very simple and something that anyone can do. That is what we see in the following story by Gary Smalley and John Trent called, "It's a Start."

There was once a wealthy family who lived in Dallas, Texas. The parents were having a very difficult time teaching their children the idea of being good stewards, to appreciate what they had and then share it with others. The children, who received everything they asked for, never considered the idea that other children did not have as much as they did. In a word, they were very spoiled.

One day, the father in the family came to the realization that his kids were living very selfish lives. Though he realized he and his wife were largely to blame, and that they should have done something years earlier, he figured that it was better late than never to steer the kids in a different direction, in a Christ-centered direction.

A week or so before Thanksgiving, the father told his family that they were going to be doing something special for the holiday. Naturally, the family immediately thought that maybe they were going to be doing something exotic like sailing in the Bahamas.

The father said, "No, this year, we're going to the downtown mission to help serve Thanksgiving dinner to some poor and homeless people."

The kids were shocked and did their best to talk him out of it. They thought their dad had gotten weird. What if their friends found out? Their friends would make fun of them for sure.

The father, however, was insistent, so the whole family went to the mission on Thanksgiving Day. What happened next, however, was something nobody in the family could have predicted. The kids could not remember when they had had a better time together as a family. They hustled around the kitchen and served up turkey and all the trimmings. They filled many cups of coffee and served pumpkin pie. They clowned around with the little kids, and they listened to the old folks tell stories of Thanksgivings they had experienced long ago and far away.

The father of the family was stunned by the reaction of his kids, but nothing could have prepared him for his kids' request a few weeks later. "Dad," they said, "we want to go back to the mission and serve Christmas dinner!"

And that is exactly what they did. The kids in the family met some of the same people they had become acquainted with at Thanksgiving. One needy family, in particular, had been on their minds. They were delighted to see that family again and spend some time with them.

Since that Christmas, the father and his family have made it a tradition to go to the mission to help during the holidays. The children of the family learned a valuable lesson. They learned how very blessed they were. They learned that it is so much better to give than to receive. They learned to be good stewards, to not only be thankful for what they had, but to share and share abundantly with those who have so little. In summary, they learned to be followers of Jesus, head of the Church.

As we enter one of the most magical seasons of the year, this story should remind us that as Catholic Christians, we should imitate Jesus. In other words, we should keep in mind that we are to see him in every human being and then act accordingly. When we train our hearts to do that, there simply isn't time in our day or room in our hearts to be selfish.

As we continue our life journeys this week, it would be a good idea to reflect on our blessings and to ask ourselves how we follow the head of our Church, Jesus Christ.

And that is the good news I have for you on this Feast of Christ the King, the last Sunday of the Church year.

Story Source: Smalley, Gary & Trent, John. "It's a Start." *Stories for the Heart: 110 Stories to Encourage Your Soul*, Ed. Alice Gray. pp. 69-70, Gresham, Oregon: Vision House Publishing Inc., 1996.

Made in the USA
Lexington, KY
05 October 2014